Letters to Dinah

Letters to Dinah

Steve Boggs

AuthorHouse™
1663 Liberty Drive
Bloomington, IN 47403
www.authorhouse.com
Phone: 1-800-839-8640

© 2011 by Steve Boggs. All rights reserved.

No part of this book may be reproduced, stored in a retrieval system, or transmitted by any means without the written permission of the author.

First published by AuthorHouse   08/13/2011

ISBN: 978-1-4634-4288-0 (sc)
ISBN: 978-1-4634-4287-3 (hc)
ISBN: 978-1-4634-4286-6 (ebk)

Library of Congress Control Number: 2011913618

Printed in the United States of America

Any people depicted in stock imagery provided by Thinkstock are models, and such images are being used for illustrative purposes only.
Certain stock imagery © Thinkstock.

This book is printed on acid-free paper.

Because of the dynamic nature of the Internet, any web addresses or links contained in this book may have changed since publication and may no longer be valid. The views expressed in this work are solely those of the author and do not necessarily reflect the views of the publisher, and the publisher hereby disclaims any responsibility for them.

I dedicate this book to the women in my life,

My oldest friend, Dinah,

My beloved Paula,

My adored girls, Carter and Cecily,

And my revered mother

With a special intention to Amy Cantor

Mais où sont les neiges d'antan?

François Villon

Do I contradict myself?
Very well then I contradict myself,
(I am large, I contain multitudes.)

Walt Whitman, "Song of Myself"

INTRODUCTION

IT WAS ON February 2nd that I received a shocking email from the husband of my oldest friend. Dinah, my friend, had lightheadedness and heart palpitations. After being rushed to the hospital it was discovered that she had a brain tumor. Yet, in the way these things go in our asynchronous age, by the time I received the information I also received several other emails detailing how Dinah's tumor was benign, that she was doing well and that her primary obstacle at this point was the tremendous challenge of recovering from brain surgery.

Living so far apart, me in South Carolina, Dinah in New York, all I could do really was to send flowers, cards and prayers. Soon enough, I spoke with Dinah's sister, Sonja, who told me that she was best in the mornings and I was able to give her a call. I cannot tell you what a relief it was to hear my friend's voice, unchanged, over the telephone. That, in and of itself, obviates any thought that email will replace voice communication.

Dinah told me that she thought that her thinking had just slowed because she had gotten old—not much of a chance of that. Dinah is a sharp cookie and I knew that was not the case. Although, with no disingenuity at all, I agreed with her that none of us are as quick as we once were, "back in the day!"

Speaking with Dinah made me reflect on how much she meant to me. Our parents were friends before we even came along and she and I and her sister Sonja had known each other our entire lives. Basically, they were the sisters that I never had but might have liked to have had. I remember one night, after their family had all come over for dinner I was having so much fun (as only a lonely, only child can understand) that I said, "Why can't Sonja and Dinah just spend the night?" I still can recall the emotional feeling in the air while the parents tried to wiggle out of this one. I always was a slow child.

In my life, my oldest friends are still my closest—I cannot account for why that is. In addition to Dinah, my two closest guy friends are Weagley and Hiser, two guys I went to elementary school with. Perhaps I feel that if people have seen you at your snake-crawling worst and still care about you, they are with you for life.

Therefore, after I spoke with Dinah I resolved to come up with a plan, a cunning one that, that Blackadder might have come up with:

Baldrick: Have you got a plan, my lord?

Blackadder: Yes I have, and it's so cunning you can brush your teeth with it.

For some reason, good or not, I decided to write a letter to Dinah each day. By this point, she had told me that her neurosurgeon wanted her to read a challenging article each day from a periodical and I figured that—while, what I would write wouldn't challenge her too much—it might amuse her. I envisioned catching her up with stories, some funny, some bittersweet, about what the years had done to me since we had spent all of our days together from elementary through high school.

What you have in your hands are the letters that I sent to Dinah during this period of recovery. Dinah is doing much better and has told me that I might share them with others. Therefore, I have put them together in this volume. If you are healthy, I hope they bring you some pleasure. If you are unwell, I hope they bring you diversion.

15 March 2009

> *"Researchers have discovered that chocolate produces some of the same reactions in the brain as marijuana. The researchers also discovered other similarities between the two but can't remember what they are."*
>
> Matt Lauer

Dear Dinah,

It has been far too long since we have really communicated, what with the crush of rearing children and with our otherwise hectic lives. However, when you head north of the 50-year mark, certain things are brought into closer focus—values, people whom you cherish, things that you wish you really had done.

One thing that I want to do is stay in closer touch with you. Perhaps like twin stars, we have each exerted a gravitational pull on each other through the years, although if that has been the case, I believe that I have probably come out the better for it. Secondly, you say that I always have some amusing stories—being a doctor certainly gives those! So, to keep you from becoming a complete couch potato, I will try to send you a good story each day.

Finally, I must say that I have tried to "write" before to no avail. The complications of plot, characterization, etc. just seem to baffle me. I would love to have that talent, but alas, or as the French more dramatically say, "Helas!", I just can't do that. But, I do seem to amuse people with my Christmas letters, so if the letters that follow bring a smile to your face, then I will have accomplished my objective.

I guess the first thing that I could tell you is that I never thought that I would reach a point in life when I was working and paying the bills and Mom was on medical marijuana. Certainly, that has to be a bit of a turn from my college days in the 70's! I must say that Mom has always had a pretty good appetite and loss of hunger has never been one of her issues. However, she has lost a good deal of weight in the past year, so as an appetite stimulant, her internist placed her on Marinol—a marijuana compound. Now, she always has the munchies.

The other night, I took her to dinner at the local Mexican restaurant. That exposed another issue, in addition to her prodigious appetite. I eat extremely quickly, in fact I wolf my food down. Not good, but a habit acquired by too many nights on call. Mom has always said, "Why do you eat so quickly?" to which I have to reply, "Because if I don't, sometimes I go hungry." In contrast, Mom loves to savor her food—a skill that I wish I had, but never have obtained. You put it in front of me and it is gone. I have never suffered through bad times like people from the depression, but if you observed me, you would probably think that I had suffered under Chairman Mao.

So, we end up going to the restaurant and I finish in something like 15 minutes. But, Mom plows through all of the various courses, decimating everything in her wake. 15 minutes for an enchilada, then a 15-minute taco. I could have used some Marinol at this point, not for the appetite effects. Endeavoring on, she finished another two items over the next 30 minutes.

But, since guilt is the water in which we all swim, I decided that first, I was not a good son for being impatient with this slow pace and secondly, I do know how she loves ice cream. So, I said, "Mom, why don't you get some ice cream?" Well, she lit up like a Roman candle and they brought out the most enormous load of chocolate, vanilla and strawberry ice cream, covered with cherries, chocolate syrup, Special K cereal and whipped cream that I have ever seen. Wincing, I settled in for the duration while she ate every individual bit of the desert over the next 45 minutes. Finally, she looked at me and said, "Steven, there is always time for ice cream."

Off the top of my head tonight, the story that comes to mind is a story that you might remember from last year's Christmas letter. However, while I will try to be more imaginative in the future, it might bring a smile to your face in the meanwhile.

I was on OB one night with the OB CRNA when one of the OB nurses came out of a room and said that she had a patient who was progressing very rapidly. She did warn us that this patient was, shall we say, not compliant. That is our nice medical term that we use for people who do not do their pre-partum testing, follow doctors advice or otherwise are just difficult.

We went into the room and this teenage girl was writhing all over the bed. Usually, this indicated time for a stern talk on my part. Consequently, I started my canned lecture, "Listen, Shanika . . . you have to really be still. We will have a needle in your back and cannot do this procedure if you are not quiet for a few minutes. If we get this epidural in, you will feel much better."

Well, Shanika didn't really see it this way. She gave me a very dirty look, rolled over on her back and hiked her right leg up in the air. The baby's

Daddy was sitting in a chair with a good view of this and said, "I think I see a head!" Suddenly, Shanika bore down with tremendous pressure and literally, the baby came out like a torpedo and flew about 2 feet, hitting the end of the bed. It would have rolled on the floor if it had not been snapped back by the umbilical cord. Coupled with this, there was a tsunami of amniotic fluid that arced across the room, leaving the room like Pucket, Thailand. Shanika's first words following delivery were to the baby's dad, "you ***, you did this to me." Hallmark moments like this are hard to capture, but Dad replied, "you ***, why don't you shut the *** up."

At this point, I could not restrain myself. I ran out of the room and I grabbed the counter at the OB desk. The nurses asked me what was going on in there and all I could get out for 10 minutes was, "baby." Every time I said more, I was overcome with paroxysms of laughter. That, coupled by the fact that every time the door opened we were treated to the endearments of Shanika and baby daddy, i.e., "you ***," sound bites eclipsed each time the door closed. So, I share with you, this season, the story of Torpedo Baby. Our own sort of Spartanburg nativity tale.

Well, Dinah, that is all for today, but as Scarlett said, "After all, tomorrow is another day." Until then, ruhig schlafen und lass nicht zu, das Bett Bugs Biss!

A pregnant lady was in an accident and she woke up in the hospital. She noticed she was not pregnant anymore and asked the nurse what happened to her baby.

The nurse said, "You have two healthy babies, a boy and a girl!"

The lady said, "Oh, I must name them," but the nurse said, "You were unconscious, so we called your brother, and he named them!"

The lady said, "But he's as dumb as a box of rocks! So what are their names?"

The nurse said, "The girl is called "Denise."

The woman replied, "Well that is a pretty name, so what did he name my boy?"

The nurse replied, "Denephew!"

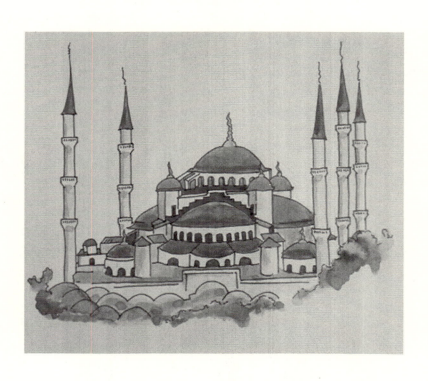

16 March 2009

> *"If one had but a single glance to give the world, one should gaze on Istanbul."*
>
> *Alphonse de Lamartine*

Dear Dinah,

    Well, I guess having writer's block after my first letter is not a very good excuse for not continuing this project, wouldn't you say! So, I thought today I would tell you what I liked about Istanbul. First, I must admit that the amount of time that we spent there was not really what I would call "in depth tourism." It was a better than just driving in a tour bus, peering out the window. But, the city—like all cities and perhaps more than most—has so many layers that knowing it well would be a long-term project.

    Since we were on a cruise, we approached the city by water, which is a remarkable way to first see it. I know that I could look at a map and say, "I saw this body of water and that one." But, truthfully, I didn't. It just seemed to me that there was water and also bridges and boats and activity everywhere. Talk about a bustle.

    Then, when our cruise liner docked, they had a Turkish band playing. To say that there was a heavy emphasis on brasses would be a kindness. And, from a cross cultural perspective, it is hard to speculate if the dissonance we heard that day is a desired aesthetic objective in that region or rather if it was the unintended consequence of the band members each having a unique idea as to where the melody should have gone. It was a close approximation to the days we shared in junior high band when Mr. Higgins would rehearse the brass section right after giving out new music, before we practiced. Nonetheless, I can state unequivocally that they individually and collectively played with an enthusiasm that I probably could not have mustered except to keep from being placed as a bauble in a Turkish bath.

    Since this was the last port of call on our cruise and also, since it was the first cruise that Paula and I have ever taken, we were unprepared for the crush of 270,000 people disembarking all at once, looking for a single taxi. However, I quickly surveyed the situation and completely without ethics, walked one street over and using my singular Turkish word, günaydın or good morning and $40.00, obtained a taxi. This caused some consternation among people who had been queued right outside of the passport gate—and would be for hours—but to smooth things over I smiled at them and mixed together a concatenation of French and Spanish and German words and my one Turkish word—held victoriously like a battle shield from the crusades. You note that I didn't use English—why give us an even worse reputation.

You would never guess that I am a planner—duh!—so I had discovered a wonderful hotel near the Four Seasons in the Sultanahmet region or old region of the city. Wonderfully, the hotel had even better views of Hagia Sophia and the Blue Mosque than the Four Seasons, but for a fraction of the price. We had lunch there and then the hotel manager had our guide meet us. I have found that if I only have a very limited period of time in a city, a private guide is well worth it and in this case it was more than true.

We happened to land in Istanbul during Ramadan, so most of the people on the tour were told or at least were under the impression that they would not be permitted to enter the Blue Mosque. Fortunately, that was not the case and our guide took us there. Outside, it is a large, physically imposing but not the most strikingly unique mosque that you have ever seen. There are what appear to be fountains or water channels along parts of the outside. This is where the observant do their ablutions or cleansings in purification prior to entering the mosque to worship. Our guide demonstrated the exact sequence of washing, including wrists, mouth, nostrils, face, arm, head and then I got lost! The amazing thing is that after years of doing this, it can be done in a matter of 30 seconds or so, especially important when it gets cold in the winter.

Entering the Blue Mosque is a transcendental experience. There is a luminescence that seems to vibrate, almost like the blue throb of electricity, through the entire structure. The only problem with that analogy is that it is too lively, in the sense that a great sense of peace and serenity descends upon you upon entry. Also, the magnitude of the structure becomes manifest, blue tiling upon blue tiling, pattern upon pattern, all compiling into a magnificent harmonic unity.

While we were there, I asked our guide to demonstrate to me the ritual prostrations that Muslims make at the time of prayer. He got down on his knees and started showing me and then said that he would show me. So, I got down next to him and Paula and I started doing the prostrations together. So, we stood, bowed with our hands on our knees, then stood up from bowing, the prostrated ourselves and did it again. Well, that caused quite a ruckus with some of the Muslim women wearing headscarves. We looked up and they were absolutely beaming. After immediate chattering between my guide and the women, the up thrust of the discussion was that they were very pleased that a visitor was interested in both learning about their religion and also in paying respect to their faith. Words do not do justice to the feeling there, but in contrast to the media images of belligerent Islamists that are always seen, this was truly a very unifying moment for me. You could see the delight in their eyes.

Well, that is all for now. More tomorrow!

> *"There is a perception among Muslims that the U.S. sees Islam as a threat . . . which sparks suspicion between one another. I hope the visit can repair ties and create a condition of mutual respect."*
>
> *Masdar Mas'udi*

17 March, 2009

> *"Wretched excess is an unfortunate human trait that turns a perfectly good idea such as Christmas into a frenzy of last-minute shopping-or attaches the name of St. Patrick to the day of the year that bartenders fear most."*
>
> Jon Anderson

Dear Dinah,

Leaving Istanbul aside for a moment let me wish you a happy St. Patrick's Day! It reminds me of when I was in the Air Force. I had a tri-service commission at the military medical school in Bethesda—I think that you visited me there once, if I am not mistaken. Anyway, my boss was a civilian, a crazy Irish woman. She used to hold up a quarter in her right hand and wave it around while talking with the phone in her left hand. This indicated to me that I was supposed to go get her a cup of coffee from the machine.

We had a wonderful secretary in the department, another Irish woman. However, the boss abused our poor secretary, using her for baby-sitting and all sorts of other personal errands. I think now, with all of the signs up for "fraud, waste and abuse," she would probably be imprisoned for her actions. However, in those days it seems like everyone turned a blind eye—like when she would take off every Thursday afternoon to go to Elizabeth Arden to have her hair done.

Speaking of hair, I remember one time she ended up going in late to Walter Reed to do some cases. She was wearing a turban. It turns out that her pilot light had gone out on her water heater and she didn't turn the gas off before deciding to relight it. So, there was a tremendous "poof" and it singed all of the hair on her brow and removed her eyebrows. After this, I took to referring to her as "Flame," which I am sure did nothing to endear me to her.

I remember distinctly talking to our secretary one day about her family. She had a large brood of Irish catholic girls. I don't remember how it came up, but she said, "all in all I must have been a success. I've reared all my girls, got them through high school and none of them are pregnant." On reflection, I think all things considered, that she did pretty well!

Speaking of St. Patrick's Day, Carter is down in Savannah, GA, to celebrate with her friends. Apparently, Savannah has a very large St. Patrick's

Day celebration. I have had variable accounts as to whether it is the second or third biggest in the country. Which leads to a new thought. Realistically, what is the point about speculating about anything anymore? I mean, I figure that New York has loads of Irish people and I know—having lived in Chicago—that they go crazy there and dye the river green and really go bonkers over the holiday. But, then again, Boston is an exemplary Irish city, too. But, what is the use? Nowadays, you just put something into Google and all of your questions are answered.

It certainly takes a lot of the fun out of it. I remember back in college and medical school when we would have long-running arguments over which city had the most of this or that, or living in South Carolina, we always said that we produced more peaches than Georgia even though they had the title as "The Peach State." To a certain point, there is something wonderful about the open-endedness of not knowing everything, not having a resolution immediately at hand. Maybe it depends on whether you like to live in uncertainty and mystery, but in my opinion, it is sort of nice to speculate as to how many species of frogs there are in the world for a while and then to maybe write off to the Bodleian to find out, rather than to have a stark figure immediately presented to you within a couple of clicks.

Inadvertently, I suspect that I have made Paula's argument for her. She does not live in the 21st century, let alone the 20th. She doesn't have email and she doesn't use a phone answering machine. You either get her or not. We tried to set up an email for her, but her friends got so frustrated with her not using it that they started emailing me. I am functionally her server/secretary/answering machine. We finally turned off the phone answering machine because people would leave messages and she would never play them, so we figured it was better for them not to think that anyone was listening instead of giving the appearance of "reception."

Admittedly, she does read the Wall Street Journal, but other than that, she concentrates on Balzac, Dostoevsky, Dickens, Jane Austin and others. I don't think that she reads anything written after 1900 and I am hard pressed to think of many things that she enjoys published after 1870. And, truthfully, I think that she is happier for all of this.

Thinking back on it, if I remember correctly, you studied German literature at Stanford. Well, let's pick something light! You and Paula would be like peas in a pod. And, Cecily. Cecily is presently rereading "Clarissa" for fun—"I have to get home tonight early so that I have a few hours to read "Clarissa", 'cause I just haven't had any good nights to read this week."

I don't know if you know it, but your family—your mother in particular—is the reason that I studied German growing up in Albuquerque, versus Spanish. Well, duh. In retrospect, I certainly think at times that I should have studied Spanish and availed myself of all of the chances to really get good at a language. I mean, I could have watched Spanish on TV and also listened to Spanish radio. But, your family and your Mom were so cool that I was just enchanted with German. Also, people always talk about German being a harsh language, but I never heard this with the way you spoke, a very soft, lilting and beautiful sound, quite melodic and charming to my ear.

Moreover, I was always mystified and jealous how your mother could tell you to get the food on the table (at least, that was my surmise) and other orders in front of company without revealing "the secret." I knew that I wanted to learn to speak another language there and then. And, while I have never really succeeded—but have tried gloriously at times, in French, German and Spanish!—I have been inspired by—as we say in that other language, Southern, y'all.

To end on an amusing note to make you smile, two stories. Our neighbor in Albuquerque was the head of the English Department at UNM. He—like me—is an avowed Francophile, but his language skills are not superior, shall we say. Once, on a canal tour in France, he was sitting across from a French woman who inadvertently knocked over her glass of wine. He wanted to say, "that's what happens when we get tipsy." However, he used the word, "ivre," meaning bald-faced drunk. Needless to say, she didn't talk with him for the rest of the night.

Another time, he spent the afternoon browsing in a French bookstore and had a short, but pleasant conversation with the owner before he left. They got along famously, until he said, "This has been a wonderful afternoon," or something to that effect. The man's demeanor changed and Pat couldn't determine why. Later, on reflection, he determined that what he had said was, "this was a highly charged erotic experience for me, too."

"till tomorrow.

In Japan, very little fat is eaten, and the heart attack rate is lower than in the USA.

In France, a lot of fat is eaten, and the heart attack rate is lower than in the USA.

In India, very little red wine is drunk, and the heart attack rate is lower than in the USA.

In Spain, a lot of red wine is drunk, and the heart attack rate is lower than in the USA.

In Brazil, people have much more sex than in Algeria, and the heart attack rate in both countries is lower than in the USA.

In conclusion:

Eat.

Drink.

Have as much sex as you'd like.

What really kills you is speaking English.

18 March 2009

> *"There's one moment with my mother that sticks out in my mind, . . . She was battling cancer. She'd already had chemotherapy and her hair was falling out. I was walking home from high school. My mother was sitting on the front porch with the radio on. She was singing a song called 'Noah, Noah' by a Latin singer named Juan Gabriel. I started singing and dancing with her, and I could see that she was happy despite the pain. That was a very special moment for me. That's the best memory I have of my mother."*
>
> *Oscar De La Hoya*

Dear Dinah,

Somewhere I must have lost a day—I went to the post office to mail a package to Paula's cousins in Berlin and discovered that it was the 18th. Not a major issue, but not working right now I don't have to particularly attend to the date. So, life has become somewhat of a flow for me. After everything that you have been through recently, I can only imagine that the same thing has happened to you. But, perhaps, to cheer ourselves up let us attribute that to age instead of anything else!

I just got back from the gym. I have tried to use this time productively and get back into shape—some sort of shape, anyway. While I workout I listen to Latino pop. I don't know why it makes me so happy, but I think there is a romanticism and lyricism that has been lost in large part in much American music. So, here I am, a middle-aged white guy doing free weights to Julieta Venegas and La 5a Estacion.

My favorite perhaps is Julieta Venegas. She has both great music, a captivating voice, plays a fierce accordion and has delightful videos. *Limon y sel* (perhaps my favorite from both a musical and a cinemagraphic point of view) is an enchanting fantasy video about a woman in love with a wolf. She loves him the way he is and faints when he discovers an elixir which makes him into a handsome "human" guy. Meanwhile, the lyrics are—despite their difficulties—that she loves him with "lemon and salt." Maybe having celebrated our 25th wedding anniversary, I appreciate that even more. I am sure Paula has seen more of the lemon and salt than sugar and spice, but thank goodness, she has tolerated me all this time.

In *Eres Para Mi*, she talks about how someone has "given her wind." Perhaps my favorite lyric is:

Lo oigo todo el tiempo
tal para cual como el mar y la sal
sigue mi cadencia
pierdo la paciencia, tú eres para mi
¿no te das cuenta?
tú eres para mi, yo soy para ti
el viento me lo dijo con un soplo suave, si.
tú eres para mi, yo soy para ti.

You took Spanish, I didn't! But, my very rough translation is:

I hear it all the time
in heaven as the sea and salt
Following my cadence.
I lose patience, you're my . . .
Do not you understand?
you are for me, I'm for you
the wind told me with a gentle murmur, yes.
you are for me, I am for you.

La 5a Estacion is much more powerfully romantic group, being whittled down to two of the original members now. Natalia Jiménez is the lead singer and it is hard not to have a crush on her—which I do, since she is so over the top. When she starts belting those songs out, she puts her soul into her music. For example, their song, *Me Murio* or "I die" is about a girl with a crush on a Luchador (one of those Mexican fighters who wear a mask or fights in lucha libre) and runs off with him. But, the entire song is about unrequited love. Imagine! They have so many other great songs, *Algo Más*, "Something More," *Daría*, "I Would Give," and *Tu Peor Error*, "Your Worst Mistake."

La Oreja de Van Gogh is another favorite—and, surprise, all of their lyrics are about unrequited love. Man, I must be on a roll! *Muñeca de Trapo*, *Rosas* and *Dulce locura* are all about crazed love.

However, they aren't all "chick groups!" Juanes is just about the coolest singer around. He is from Columbia and I used to love to listen to him. Then, one evening I saw him on "Austin City Limits." What a performer!

He has such a powerful and yet subtle voice, and on stage he has an incredible presence. He seems to cross the language barrier quite easily. He tried to make it in L.A. by imitating other styles and finally settled on his own hybrid mixture of rock and roll and Latin.

La Camisa Negra (Black Shirt) is about how his life went down the tubes (I've got a black shirt), but it got banned several places because some fascists adopted it. He actually had to come out and state that it had nothing to do with fascism! The video is just amusing, with two gorgeous women dancing while an elderly Mexican guy plays a detached guitar. The result is a "wave" of music that sweeps across the city, causing everyone to dance in rhythm to the song. In *Me Enamora* he gets to show off his guitar capabilities—he plays a Fender Stratocaster—and in *Para Tu Amor* he gets to show off his lyricism.

I could go on and on about these groups all day. Strange fruit for a guy who really considers Mozart as his first love. Perhaps, it is something about growing up in New Mexico that makes these sounds resonate in my soul. Or, as I alluded to earlier, it might be the more "shirt on your sleeve" romanticism that all of these singers seem to embrace that has captured my love.

My final recommendation, in a very long list, is Alex Syntex. He has a song entitled, *Intocable*. The lyrics are about love, but the song and video seem to have a more powerful message about moral blindness. He has people walking helplessly around large plazas with sunglasses, seeking help, as if they have all suddenly suffered from a disease, which has afflicted the entire population at one time.

I believe that it was filmed in the Zócalo in Mexico City, at least judging from glimpses that I see on the video of a cathedral that looks like the cathedral there. The blind people in the video seem to be gravitating to video monitors and also to the singer—one of the only sighted people in the video—looking for direction. Perhaps, only our singers, poets and other artists can give us moral direction?

Well, that's it for today! Bis spatter! Or, today should I say, hasta mañana?

"I find there's always something to do in Mexico City, at any hour."

Michael Roberts

19 March 2009

> *My feet ain't got nothing to do with my nickname, but when folks get it in their heads that a feller's got big feet, soon the feet start looking big.*
>
> *Satchel Paige*

Dear Dinah,

Since you haven't ever lived in the South, you probably aren't familiar with the phenomenon of "names." It wasn't until we moved to Gaffney that I learned that grown men would completely, appropriately and without either reservation, perjoration or humor be referred to as "Frog," "Sweetback," or "Onion."

These names many times are acquired at a very young age and stay with you for life. For example, our mayor is named, "Chicken Jolly." The first time Paula and I learned this, we saw a cartoon in the local paper over some budget item with a caption like, "Chicken Jolly—still no guts." We thought, "Wow, these local papers get pretty personal."

Later at one of the local watering holes, we saw Henry Jolly and asked him about it and he told us that, well, yes the attacks were personal but the nickname came from his childhood. I don't remember exactly what he did to earn that moniker—I will have to check that out, now that I think about it—but originally at least it did not refer to his degree of courage!

Speaking of chickens, though, makes me think of one of our neighbors. She was a naughty little girl growing up and one day her Dad put her in charge of the chickens while he went to town. Who knows where children come up with these ideas but for some reason she decided that it would be a barrel of laughs to stick frogs (yes, frogs) down the throats of the chickens and see what would happen.

She started off slow, with one chicken, stuffing a frog down the chicken's throat. Well, the chicken—can a chicken turn blue?—jumped all around the yard and literally ran around like it didn't have a head (since, I guess it didn't have much oxygen going there) and put on quite a show, running into things and falling over.

So, our ever-indefatigable girl kept going (I don't know if she used the same frogs over or used a new one for each chicken!). But, needless to say, she definitely put a dent in the number of chickens that her Daddy had before he returned.

This was before the days of social services and I believe that she couldn't sit down for several days. I am sure in the new age of federalism, someone, somewhere is trying to figure out a way to prosecute this long-dead man for violations of some child protection policy. Boo.

To make a not so subtle segue from chickens to frogs, there is a guy in town named, "Toad," too. Now, admitted this goes well back before my time so I have to rely on some of my friends. Poor Toad had a very difficult life, seeing his father murder his mother in front of him. So, he was never quite right from the git-go. But, he has done yard work for us and—how do you put it, like a bad reference—under strict supervision, is able to function adequately.

In high school, they had a talent assembly where everyone could do their own little performance. I imagine—just like you and Barbara Search—there were the good girls playing the flutes and probably some guys trying to do some basically edgy stuff, but all the time knowing that it "is" a high school and that they do want to graduate. Well, this all did not register on Toad. Hear tell, he got them to play, "Do what you wanna do," and then started prancing around on the stage, thrusting and grabbing his crotch pre-Michael Jackson, then lay on the stage and started air humping. As you can imagine, this really took 1970's Gaffney by storm! I don't know how long it took for them to get the hook, but I am almost positive that it took only long enough for the neural impulses of what was happening to register in the brains of the teachers and then for the efferent impulse to be created and to get the hook.

Actually, Toad has worked in our yard—under strict supervision. One time, I asked a bunch of guys to go behind our fence where we have some cypresses and clean out some of the underbrush and other stuff. None of them would do it, telling me that there were probably snakes and other things back there. Toad got really agitated over this and started jumping around like he was possessed (as I said, works well under supervision!). His eyes rolled and he started screaming, "Snake charmer, snake charmer. I take care of it, I AM the snake charmer." So, what the heck. We all let Toad go clean out the underbrush and thankfully there were no snakes and he did not have to use his special powers—what is that power that Harry Potter has that lets him understand snakes? Toad must have Parseltongue. I am sure that Toad, Harry and the snakes could have quite a party.

Lest you think that names are the only thing of note, however (and, in future letters I have many more stories about names!), personal stories are always a reliable source of interest here. For example, one person who has done work for us was disconsolate because his marriage failed. Sympathetically, I tried to lend an ear and see how I could support him in this difficult period. As it turned out, the story was slightly more complicated than that.

Yes, for reasons that will probably never be clear and remain in the darkened pools of the relationships between two people, his marriage did not work. However, he did not do what I would have done if I were reading books like, "Can this marriage be saved?" He took up with her sister and started living with her. However, living marginally without much income, there was not—shall we say—a lot of disposable income to go around. And, this was well before the current economic meltdown.

What to do, what to do? Hum. Well, there is only one solution. Get a second doublewide and put it up a stone's throw across from your wife's trailer, but on the same property, so that you don't have to pay additional rent. Then, have some more kids. But, last I saw him, he is still happy and doing well. I must admit, however, that except for asking, "how is the family," I now longer seek more specific clarification.

Well, I guess that is all that I've got for today! Hope you are feeling well.

TTYL,

Stop Inbreeding! Ban country music.

Daryl Ganskopp

20 March 2009

> *One thing they never tell you about child raising is that for the rest of your life, at the drop of a hat, you are expected to know your child's name and how old he or she is.*
>
> Erma Bombeck

Dear Dinah,

    Today I got up and looked at my calendar and I see that Thomas Cranmer, a martyr of the Anglican Church, was burned at the stake this day in 1556. It makes me think how far we have come as Episcopalians, from having a core of beliefs for which we would be willing to subject ourselves willingly to such a fate. Presently, Episcopalians are parodied by Eddie Izzard and Betty Butterfield (and very well, I must say—they are hilarious!) for their spinelessness and lack of conviction. And, too much kneeling. I suspect that all you have to do is look to the Archbishop of Canterbury to see where the problem lies.

    Speaking of history, I know this is a significant year for you with Julia starting her first year at Harvard. And, while you must be tremendously proud of her, I am sure that the change is disconcerting in some ways. The summer before Carter started at UVA, she worked at Cracker Barrel as a waitress—and a very good one, I might add. So, come the fall, Paula and I obligatorily collected her stuff in the SUV and migrated like so many other parents on the interstate highways, like the people in Steinbeck's "Grapes of Wrath," looking for better situations (getting the kids out of the house).

    I discovered at that point that parents are invited only for one reason. To schlep stuff up to dorm rooms. There were all these fit and buff and athletic college boys standing around, obviously surveying the incoming college girls. However, far be it from them to break a sweat—no, they were too busy posturing and keeping their hair groomed to lift anything. So, like all the other beleaguered fathers, I was out there jockeying with the other dads, faking each other out, trying to get the closest parking space to the dorms. Ha! No, I am not pulling out, just getting more stuff.

    So, we took pictures of Carter with all the girls in her suite and her roommate and knew that these would be best friends for life—not. And, then we videoed her walking away from our car as she left us to go up to the dorm. (So incredibly pathetic, I know). And, then we hit the road.

And, being a good husband, I was so worried about Paula, who was lost in some Balzac novel or something as we are driving. She is oblivious to everything, but I just want to reassure her that things will be O.K. So, I say, "Don't worry, she will be fine." Paula nods. "Everything will be fine; we have Cecily for another year." Paula nods.

This continues for several miles and then—perchance—we pass a Cracker Barrel sign. And, I don't know what happened or overcame me but I just burst into tears. I guess that it all hit me. My daughter would never again be *in* my house in the same way. She was growing up, if not grown up to a certain degree. She might come home again for holidays and time between jobs and other such things, but life had taken for us as a family an irreversible, earthshaking change.

Well, Paula at first thought I was having a heart attack. In retrospect, I guess it was so funny. I didn't want to cry, so I just put on my sunglasses but that only made it worse. So, finally I had to pull over to the side of the road and get over it. Then we decided that—at that point at least—Paula had been the primary caregiver for the girls and boy, she was relieved that Carter was going to be independent! Not that she loved her less or anything like that, but she was fatigued (generous word) of the daily friction of living with a teenage daughter. So, what she viewed as liberation I was pathetically sick over. Needless to say, over the years, those roles have oscillated back and forth several times, but at least that day, I was the basket case.

I must admit that when we took Cecily to Rice—road trip!—it was a different experience. First, I will never, never, never drive to Houston again from S.C. It is as far to Houston as it is to Boston from S.C. Texas is such a big state that it should just be illegal, but then again, I guess if they did that, they would have to put the state to death. The A.C.L.U would never allow that, except maybe *for* Texas. So, we had—again—so much stuff in our Range Rover (made me want my Suburban back) that Carter was in the front seat and little Cecily was like a bug in the back seat, wedged between all of her stereo equipment, books, book cases, CD's, shoes, clothes, etc. I would have gone stark raving mad having so few degrees of freedom for a two-day drive.

But, the good news was that at Rice—the geekie, tech campus, there were all these nice, helpful boys who helped unpack our stuff. Lovely. And, I will say another thing. Compared to losing my first child, I was so happy, delighted, and giddy to drop Cecily off. She was so despondent after Carter left, being alone in the house, that we didn't see her that much anyway. She was always, "out at the lake with friends," or "at school," or "with so and so." I guess that God has a way of preparing even fools such as yours truly for the next stage of life.

It is amazing, but with the passage of time, I had forgotten why Paula didn't go with us to take Cecily to school. That summer, the girls were studying French in Montreal and that was when we got the diagnosis of Paula's breast cancer. To tell you how something like that is so overwhelming, at first she didn't even think of bringing them home. Needless to say, calmer heads—mine—prevailed and I said, "of course they need to be here for you." But, thinking back on that period, that was why Paula couldn't go with us—she was getting chemo while we took Cecily out to school.

One thing wonderful about our little town is that we have had such support. I know that when I was gone with the girls, but even more when I got back and had to continue working and taking call, etc., neighbors and friends took care of everything in our lives for something like 4 months. I know specifically that without organizing anything, for 4 months I didn't cook a single meal. The women in Paula's luncheon club got together and made their own schedule and—so they wouldn't disturb her in the afternoon—would put a fully-cooked meal on a T.V. tray on our front porch.

I think that this might not meet the theological criteria of Thomas Cranmer or other Catholic or Protestant or even Islamic or Jewish zealots. However, if you take as your primary commandment the injunction that "of these, love is the greatest," I think that all of the women who took care of Paula, god in whatever manifestation, is smiling generously upon them. And, while I cannot be with you to hold your hand and do things for you, I hope that my letters are bringing a small smile to your face.

> *"You get these small-town feuds because people don't have cablevision. You don't have anything else to do."*

Michael Bobick

March 21, 2009

> *"I want death to find me planting my cabbages, but caring little for it, and even less for my imperfect garden"*
>
> *Michel de Montaigne*

Dear Dinah,

Our house has been in an uproar over the transition/move, whatever you want to call it that we are undergoing, with my new position in Pennsylvania. We have decided to keep our house in South Carolina to ultimately retire back to. However, the exercise of having to go through the detritus which has accumulated over 20 years is both useful and fatiguing. Having always been one to hold on to every paper in case I need it later, I have been spending a lot of quality time with my shrewder. And, I remember that Mother Teresa said that, "if you haven't worn it is the past year, it belongs to the poor" If that really is the case, I have been holding out on them for quite a while. I won't say that they will be "styling" if they wear some of the things that I am turning over, but hopefully they will be warm, well shod and comfortable. Albeit in colors and patterns that fashionistas would use in evidence against me in any good competency hearing.

Another thing that I have had to do is find and train someone to care for our yard. I know that sounds rather prosaic, but in point of fact, it is a much more complicated issue than it appears on the surface. Originally, Paula and I were charmed by formal French gardens and thought, "boy, no grass, no lawn mower—that has to be easy to take care of." I do not know what planet I was on when I thought that or which beverage I was imbibing (a fine Bordeaux, perhaps?). Actually, through time and painful experience, I have learned that a well trimmed, parterre garden is probably one of the most time-intensive landscapes that you can plant.

Over time I have grown both to love my garden and spending time with it. It is an almost Zen-like experience, shaping and sculpting the plants. I do have to use power tools, because I do not have infinite time. I simply cannot live in Zeno's paradox. But, I have it down to a routine. First, for the parterres, I smooth the tops, being careful not to go too low because if you do that the leaves burn in the summer. But, if you don't trim enough, the boxwood gets "leggy" and doesn't retain its sculptural characteristic.

Then, I move to the outside of each parterre, making sure that there are not errant branches or leaves. After this, I do the inside of each "box" within the parterre—there are 4 outside parterres and one circle in the middle. To cap it off, I then take the edger and slightly touch up the corners along the outside and inside of the parterres so that when seen from across the garden, you don't see any strays. Finally, Paula usually comes and takes a broom and knocks off all of the loose leaves from the boxwood with brings up some extra stuff for me to trim. All of this can be done in a morning, but this is my "golf game."

However, the hedges are another matter. I used to go to work and tell people that I was tired on Monday because I trimmed the hedges over the weekend. People would either look at me like I was a wimp (maybe) or they would be perplexed or they would just roll their eyes. Then, we had a few parties and people saw that my hedges were 25-30 feet high. I started with a hedge trimmer with an extension, then I ended up using this in conjunction with a 14-foot ladder, standing on top of the ladder with the hedge trimmer. Believe me, compared to going to the YMCA, it is a really good upper body workout! After a weekend of "trimming the hedges," my shoulder girdle is sore and aching.

So, now since we will be living in Pennsylvania primarily, I am training people to care for my plants. It's funny—I have worked with medical residents in the past and I guess there is a more general body of knowledge of medicine that I assume that we are all working from. That—to a certain degree—gives me less anxiety. Of course, I say this in part tongue in cheek. But, for the yard you just can't take someone and let him or her free with a clipper—they can destroy the growth of 20 years in a few hours. It would be like letting a medical student do an operation. There are so many subtle little things that you don't think to say, that are implicit, in gardening. Just like in medicine.

This Monday, I spent the day flying to Mississippi to be fingerprinted. Before I start my job in Pennsylvania, I had hoped to do some temporary assignments in the Carolinas. However, the economy is so terrible that there is no temporary work anywhere in either North or South Carolina. So, surprisingly even to me, I will be a Mississippi doctor for the month of April.

Getting medical licenses is not easy (appropriately so), since they go back to every hospital that you have ever worked in, even 30 years ago. Moreover, recently I was surprised when I applied for my Pennsylvania license. I got a letter stating that I could not apply for a new Pennsylvania medical license that I had to reactivate my old Pennsylvania license. That amazed me because I forgot that I had one—the last time I used it was when I was in training at Penn in 1986. Actually, it is easier to reactivate, but it was just a surprising situation. Likewise, I forgot that I had an Illinois license, because that was a training license and I never practiced in the state. I was not trying to be disingenuous, but believe me, that was a long time ago!

Cecily is currently in San Francisco visiting with an old friend. Dima (for Dmitri) is a Russian kid from Seattle whom Carter and Cecily met in Tours, France when they were studying there in middle school. The first summer they were in France, Dima liked Cecily and she had a boyfriend. The second summer, he likewise missed the boat and she had a boyfriend. Finally, the third year, he planned to get there early and preempt the fact that she might get a boyfriend. However, for some reason, he got delayed and by the time he got to Tours, a couple of days late—alas!—Cecily had yet a new boyfriend. Carter thought that this was just about the funniest state of affairs, always being amused by the travails of Cecily's boyfriends.

Carter is home with us for the weekend. She spent St. Patrick's Day in Savannah—and was depressed that contrary to rumor, they did not dye the river green like they do in Chicago. She went down with a bunch of kids from school and then we are the proud beneficiaries of the tail end of spring break. So, there has been much talking and watching of movies and going out to dinner—nothing fancy, but it is great to have her home.

I wanted to let you know that Paula and I loved the Anniversary Card—thank you so much! It was wonderful to receive it. In addition, I must say that your writing is still as strong and beautiful as it has ever been. I have always been impressed by how you do that. I have to type my letters because I want people to be able to read them. However, I was reared to believe that a handwritten note is the most personal and exquisite gift and you pass the superlative mark there. But, if you get a letter in Chinese characters from Gaffney, look again—it is probably just my bad writing!

> *"Envy is what makes you, when an acquaintance is lustily telling you that she's dating a Greek god of a guy, ask, 'Which one, Hades?'"*
>
> Regina Barreca

22 March 2009

> *"If you don't know where you are going, any road will get you there."*
>
> Lewis Carroll

Dear Dinah,

 Today I was thinking about blindness of various sorts. I don't know if you know it, but Paula is as blind as a bat. No, really. In Chicago, years ago, she and her roommate from college were walking downtown and Paula was bumped at about shoulder level. So, of course she said, "excuse me!' Allison looked at her incredulously and said, "you know that you just excused yourself to a parking meter, don't you!"

 On another occasion, Paula was taking the "L" or "elevated" back from a late meeting at Sears. The platform was deserted and she was by herself, standing in the middle where the train would arrive. Then, with a pretty good amount of time before the train was expected, a sketchy guy showed up and started looking at her. (I just love that word. I don't know if it is still "operative"—it was big about 7 years ago when Carter started college and not being au courant, I am sure that the cognoscenti have moved on, but I will just stay with "sketchy." But, I digress).

 So, Paula—at that time younger, more naive and less assertive—looked straight ahead and pretended that he wasn't there. Undeterred, he edged closer to her. So, all the time pretending that she was not paying attention to him, she moved further along the platform. He followed. She would move and he would follow. They continued this unscripted choreography until finally, she had reached the wall at the end of the platform. What to do, what to do?

 Suddenly, Paula felt a "tap, tap, tap" on her hand. So, almost reflexively—and remembering her myopia—she bent over to see what was tapping her. Needless to say, Dorothy, our city girl found herself looking straight into this guy's erection. Fortunately for both parties, I suspect, the train arrived at just that moment and Paula was saved from further perdition by the closing door of the train. Within the family, this is known as "Mommy's tap-tap-tap" story.

 Within Gaffney, initially at first, some people didn't understand that Paula was really as blind as she is. You have got to understand that in a small town, everyone waves to everyone—sometimes if you don't know them but particularly if you do. To put it delicately, Paula is a focused driver. She backs out of the driveway, peers down the road and her eyes do not veer to either left or right. She is fanatically intent on straight ahead.

So, when you pass people and they wavy—at least in these parts—people may think that you are snobbish or aloof or what all. The only saving grace in Paula's case is her maniacal consistency. Everyone now knows that she can't see since she has passed so many people—including me, my mom, and our rector among others—and not even acknowledged them. So, I believe the general consensus now is just, "Oh, there goes Paula. Glad she missed me."

There are other types of blindness which I am sad to say are less excusable. Because we took our cruise in the fall and because I don't start my new job until May, we decided not to go overboard for our anniversary this year. But, when I was in San Diego I found the most exquisite painting by a new favorite artist, Tim Cantor. To describe it very briefly, it is a mixed media work of an absolutely stunning, exquisitely beautiful young woman wearing a turban. I saw this work in the artist's gallery and I knew at that moment that I had to have it. Since our 25th anniversary was coming up, I arranged to have it shipped out for our anniversary.

Everyone who has seen this picture has thought it was absolutely exquisite. Carter found it magnificent. However, Paula—while she likes it—I know her well enough to know that there was something else going on, that she was processing something else because she wasn't just raving about the picture.

Well, there are ways that I read pictures and that you read pictures and then there are ways that others read them. I have not been completely forthright in my description of the painting, either. Because, you see, in the painting I focused on the wonderful execution of the young woman and the fabric and all of those details. However, over in the right corner there is the hand of time coming in to touch her. To me, this was merely incidental to the primary focus of the painting. However, to give this to a woman for your 25th anniversary is not what I would call, what would the word be? Sensible? Intelligent? Sensitive?

So, after 25 years of a good marriage with someone, I am still capable of pulling out the emotionally insensitive, male blind act. I have completely forsworn getting art for anyone in the family for holidays. The girls still don't let me live down the fact that one year following Paula's breast cancer diagnosis we were in Mexico and I got her a very expensive and beautiful "Tree of Death." Even as I put this down, it sounds so much worse that it was intended. It is just a fabulous work that we still have in our library. But, like the young boy who buys his Mom a football for her birthday, I have got to get to the point where I just buy these things for myself. It is a character defect that I need to work on.

I do know my salvation, however. Jewelry. Except for these two bone-headed mistakes in the art category, I have had a very good track record as a husband, but this was by buying jewelry that Paula likes. And, the nice thing about jewelry is that there is typically no worry about how to "read it," or "what does it mean to you." It just is there and can be played with. Tanzanite, beautiful costume jewelry, semi-precious jewels, you name it—it doesn't even have to be expensive so much, but it definitely keeps you out of trouble!

I might add that I am not the only one who has made the "gift mistake." One day, I was in the library reading and I heard all this noise on the front porch. I looked out and didn't see anyone there. But, there were two antique chairs there. And, coming up the walk, with two more chairs, one under each arm, was Paula. I looked at her and said, "What are these?" Beaming, she said, "These are your birthday present." I looked at her like she was out of her mind. Starting to demure, she gave me a very stern look and said, emphatically, "These are your birthday present. I don't want to hear anything more about it." And, she didn't. I love those chairs.

Here are the top twenty mistakes males make when giving gifts to women. Make any one of them to your peril.

A BAD Gift is any gift that:

1. Plugs in. (It depends—see gift-giving rules.)

2. Reminds her of a former relationship. (Always.)

3. Says, you were too busy to be creative. (Shame on you.)

4. Is really for your benefit and not hers. (Gotcha.)

5. Says, she is getting old. (Head for the hills, bucko.)

6. Says, she is not as beautiful as the day you met her. (You will be sleeping alone a lot from now on.)

7. Is re-packaged in any way. (I am not even going to give this one any energy.)

8. Looks like you were being cheap. (If you were, make sure you are with yourself as well.)

9. Reminds you of a former relationship of yours. (What are you, just plain stupid?)

10. Says, she needs to lose a little weight. (Ditto, no. 9 above.)

11. You believe will make her life easier. (Did you just land here from some distant planet?)

12. Lacks romance. (Better read Romance 101 again.)

13. Says, you really don't know me. (You are history, bubba.)

14. Says, you are guilty of something. (If you are, gifts are not going to do it for you here, dude; better consider just fessing up.)

15. Tries to buy your way out of the doghouse. (Just learn to be happy there.)

16. Says, she is not the center of your world. (You better get a new girl friend.)

17. Helps her be more successful in her career. (This one could be a little touchy, boys.)

18. Helps her with her domestic responsibilities. (Big freaking deal.)

19. Shows your general lack of thoughtfulness. (Your mother will not be happy about this one.)

20. Originates from motives that are less than honest. (You are not fooling anyone.)

Tim Connor

23 March 2009

Fashion is a form of ugliness so intolerable that we have to alter it every six months.

Oscar Wilde

Dear Dinah,

I am sitting in the airport restaurant in Jackson, Mississippi writing this letter to you. Since I hope to do some temporary work in Mississippi in April, I had to come to the Medical Board here to be fingerprinted and then to take an open-book jurisprudence exam. The technology that they use is really cool for the fingerprinting. Compared to when I was fingerprinted in the Air Force, with ink that smeared all over everything, the methodology now is water-based. You put your finger and/or fingers in water and then on a screen—depending on whether they are doing individual prints or full "hand prints." The images are captured digitally on computer (imagine—what isn't!). It still takes 24-48 hours for them to get their report back, so I hope those ax murders from Mrs. Sorsby's class in 7th grade are expunged by now.

What to write, what to write. Well, you know that I do swim in a sea of estrogen. Growing up, I was always with Mom because Dad was always at work. And, then after marriage to Paula the girls came along in short order. We thought that we would pick an androgynous name for our first, i.e. Carter, so that she would not be discriminated against when people would read her stationary. Carter Bailey Boggs, Esq. Well, I guess if you don't go for mauve or pink, it could be a guy.

With Cecily, however, Paula's inner girl worked triumphantly to the fore. I guess by that point she was convinced that either women had advanced enough in society that they could have feminine names or else that she (Paula) really didn't give a flying fig. So, we picked Cecily and people adore it. In fact, we get compliments on both of the girls' names. Not like when I was growing up in first grade. There you didn't yell either "fire' or "Steve," because it would cause a riot. There were 6 "Steves" in my first grade class. I still rue the fact that I didn't get to keep Stevens, which I really what I was supposed to be called, after a favorite branch of the family. So much more distinguished. Ha.

I note this all as a preface to the fact that if British monarchs can claim to rule by divine right, I can claim to know something about women just by osmosis. Therefore, when some of my female technicians at the hospital started telling me about some of the parties that they were going to go to, my ears picked up. I just couldn't resist asking them what they were going to wear. So, they told me that they had "this" in mind for a given spring party and "that" in mind for another formal occasion.

Well, I just rolled my eyes and said, "Girls, no, that just will not work." So, they asked me what I would recommend. And, having been through this type of routine in my personal life ad infinitum and ad nauseum, I said, "You really need to keep it simple. You need to start with a L.B.D. Then, just have some simple sling backs. Only wear simple diamond stud earrings and do your hair in a chignon." They all looked at me, stunned, and then, one of them took my hand and said, "Dr. Boggs, you know, you really need to spend more time with guys." So, they took my advice and I have subsequently taken theirs.

Women can be the death of you, in more than one way. Our house is well north of 100 years in age and another house close to us is even older. It used to be owned by a judge who ended up in a nursing home for moderate dementia. Now, this judge was very proper, never one to curse or act out or do anything improper. I believe that he was a deacon in his church—and, I say that knowing that deacons have been known to act out. But, he was not one of those.

Well, it turns out that his wife died and he was a widower for several years, living quietly without any disturbances before his dementia required that he be placed in—comment dites-on?—assisted living. Once in assisted living, however, he became something of a wild man. The nursing aides would find him in bed with this old lady or that old lady and they couldn't pry them apart with crowbars. Try as they might, they just couldn't keep them separated.

So, the only solution that the nursing home could come up with was to have his son talk to him. Dutifully, his son went to talk to his Daddy about being, how shall we put it, more age appropriate. I do not know how you initiate a discussion such as this. I mean, you expect to discuss this stuff with your kids, but your parents? But, his son worked his courage up and broached the subject. His father's reply? "I can't give it up. I've just got to have it." After that, the son figured that this Daddy was paying good money for the nursing home and if they had a problem with it, they could deal with it. But, women will make you crazy. At any age.

I know that this elderly gentleman and one of his "beaus" from the nursing home also tried to escape and run off in her car for some afternoon delight. Unfortunately, they forgot that her car had been sold years earlier and therefore their escape was truncated.

With dementia, you either have to laugh or you would just be very sad and depressed over the loss of a person's faculties. Therefore, when I share with you some of the incidents that I have experienced with Mom, now that she has entered that progressive decline, I do it because I know that you know her and would be both interested and concerned about her welfare. Perhaps, most importantly however, she has entered a very happy stage lately and never seems to be upset and angry over things—we went through that phase a while ago and it was particularly difficult.

The guy who lives on the other side of us is a tall, big guy and is several years my junior. He is not married but does have a girlfriend. And, he is a very friendly type of guy, who speaks to everyone, including Mom and sometimes they have had the chance to chat. The other day, Paula and I were over chatting with Mom (her house is right across the street from ours—I think you knew that) and our neighbor's name came up. Mom said, "You know, looking back on it, I think I should have been nicer to him" So, obligatorily, Paula and I said, "Why, what did you do to him?"

So, Mom followed up with, "Oh, I didn't *do* anything bad. But, just thinking back on it, he was awfully friendly when I moved to town. And, now I think that maybe if I had been friendlier, well, you know." So, blankly, Paula and I still said, "No, what do you mean." And, then she blurted out, "Well, I think that he was interested in me as a woman and we might be married if I had been a little more friendly."

There was absolutely no, and I mean NO, movement of air in that room for the next few moments—probably just a few seconds, but they seemed interminable. Truthfully, Paula and I were so stunned that I am sure neither of us remembers how the conversation changed. I mean, what do you use as a segue from that. Well, your daffodils are really looking good now, Kathy!"

So, that's my letter for today. I just received my check from my server. Her name is Cyndi. I wonder if she puts hearts or circles over "I" in her name.

"I used to be Snow White, but I drifted."

Mae West

24 March 2009

> *"I think I'm more grounded, you know, and I know what I want out of life and I'm, you know, my morals are really, you know, strong and I have major beliefs about certain things and I think that has helped me, you know, from being, you know, coming from a really small town."*
>
> *Britney Spears*

Dear Dinah,

I don't know why I was thinking about it this morning, but I was reflecting on how different the paths we have taken. I mean, you have lived in some spectacular cities—Munich, Palo Alto, San Francisco, Boston and New York and summered in the Hamptons! Wow—what a delight! I have lived in some great cities, too, like Chicago and Philly, but I guess that if you stack them up, superficially they just don't compete.

But, maybe having lived in the South long enough, I am "Faulkneresque" enough to actually thrive on my place in the sun. Like Thoreau said, "I have traveled much in Concord." I read for intellectual stimulation and travel for inspiration and for art. But, for people I seem to get it here, in my own little Petri dish.

When I first moved to Gaffney, I remember that I was looking for a place to have breakfast. You have to remember that 20 years ago, Gaffney was not even as up-town as it is today. So, after much exploration and asking some people, I found that there was a diner downtown. I went there one weekday and it was like going back—even then—30 years, now more like 50. There were those old stainless-steel display and serving cabinets—like we used to have in middle school. They had the "Jesus music" playing—Lordy, I don't know the songs, but I recognize them when I hear them. And, the woman who came to serve me had a beehive that was taller than any that I had ever seen before.

So, she directed me to a table in the middle of the room and I sat down. She gave me a menu, which I had time to look over while she gave me some perfectly brewed old-fashioned coffee. The prices were amazing. I think that I ordered something like 3 eggs sunny side up, 3 sausage, hash browns, orange juice and the coffee all for $3.00. I am sure the prices are higher now.

But, then I looked at her and said, "And, I would like some white toast." She looked at me askance, and thinking that she might not have either heard me or understood me, I repeated, "So, may I please have some white toast?" She shook her head vigorously, and said, "You know that we can't do that!" When I asked her why, she said—with truly no irony intended—"because, when we toast it, it turns brown." Now, I can guarantee that you don't have *that* in Rye!

Another time, one of the hospital administrators returned from Charlotte after the evening there with his wife. She was pregnant and therefore had some of those particular tastes that accrue to someone in that condition. They dropped by Burger King to get her a burger—the only place open in those days at that time—and she really wanted just a plain hamburger. So, that was the order that they placed—a "plain hamburger." Well, that really threw the girl behind the counter. She said, "You don't want no mustard on that burger?" To which they replied, "No." She asked, "You don't want no ketchup or pickles on that burger?" Obligingly, they said, "No." Going down the list of things, finally the girl got so exasperated and confused that she said, "You don't want no meat on that burger?"

However, it would be a misimpression should I suggest that everyone here is like that. The wonderful thing about our small town is that we have a writer in our neighborhood, several artists, and some really shrew intelligent people. I think that it is just the scale and scope where we live that is so different from when Paula and I lived in larger cities. Certainly, time is a much more elastic phenomenon here than elsewhere.

When I first moved to town, I remember sitting behind two women at a traffic light. They were conversing, digging in their purses and playing around in my opinion. Well the light had changed and I did not really want to sit through another round. So, I honked my horn. Little did I know that basically the horn has one primary function in Gaffney—it serves as a way of saying, "Hey!" to your friends. So, both of these women turned around and waved to me sweetly. Talk about comeuppance!

Regarding these letters, I hope that they have brought some amusement to your days. Carter was home this weekend—at the end of her spring break—and we were talking about correspondence. Letter writing seems to be such a lost art that it can seem somewhat frivolous or non-significant in today's world. However, Carter was emphasizing to me that there is a very long tradition in French literature of the significance of letter writing, correspondence, whatever you want to call it. And, sitting in our garden having coffee with Paula this morning, she said the same thing applies to

English literature. And, also the bible, with Paul's letters among others. So, I guess we should call these, "Steve's letters to the Howlands!"

Moreover, I can't think of anything more personal to give someone than both some of your thoughts and time. In a world where you can basically surf the Internet and find a gift for someone on Amazon or any other online vendor, it is not hard to send a thoughtful and material present. But, trying to sit down and synthesize a bit of your life for someone—that is of an entirely different magnitude.

Additionally, there is the risk of running out of things to say. Heretofore, I haven't hit the wall (or, if I have, you have been kind enough not too tell me!). And, then there is the necessity for some degree of reflection and introspection. I feel that presently it is so easy to be overwhelmed by the noise and distraction in the world that we never have a chance to sit down and actually enjoy the smaller moments.

In my limited travels in poorer countries, especially Mexico, I find that although materially impoverished, people seem to have time for each other. I would never go so far as to idealize poverty and say that that is "the way to live." But, on the other hand, perhaps we do have some lessons to learn from people who live with less and spend more time focused on each other. I say this sitting writing on my computer ;)

So, I digress—perhaps I have hit the wall for today. Bis spatter!

> *Yesterday is a dream, tomorrow but a vision. But today well-lived makes every yesterday a dream of happiness, and every tomorrow a vision of hope. Look well, therefore to this day.*
>
> *Sanskrit Proverb*

25 March 2009

> *If I had to choose between betraying my country and betraying my friend,*
> *I hope I should have the guts to betray my country.*
>
> E. M. Forester

Dear Dinah,

Perhaps it is the fact that I will be moving or it might be the changes that I have been through lately. Whatever the case, I have been musing on the nature of friendship, its fragility and effervescence. It seems like when you have it, it is so easily taken for granted and when it is gone, it leaves a gaping rent in your life.

Last night, I had to say goodbye to a group of people with whom I have meet several times a week for almost a decade. We have usually gotten together and shared our stories, with an unusual degree of frankness for this day and age. Someone is usually dealing with some sort of problem and while we tend to avoid solving problems for each other, we do talk about how we have managed similar situations.

I have been friends with some of the people in this group for over 9 years now and it is amazing the changes which we have all gone through. Divorces. Job losses. Problems with children. In my case Paula's breast cancer. Certainly, sharing your burdens with friends does make the path easier. For someone like me, who tends to protect an inner core, this has been a transformative experience. Having people whom you can rely and depend upon, who you know have your best interest at heart, really makes life a wonderful journey.

Conversely, in stark contrast to this group is my experience with most of the people with whom I worked daily for almost 20 years at the hospital. Since I have left the hospital, I can count on a few hands (sic) the number of people who have written to wish me well and to give me good wishes. The cardiac surgeons, most of the nurses and technicians and actually a very large number of patients have spoken to me. However, for example, none of the orthopedic surgeons with whom I worked have taken the time to write or even call.

I think that this might be reflective of our age, where people are considered "disposable" to a certain degree. Once you are out of sight, once you cannot do something for them, you are not important, not significant, not worth the time or bother. I do not think that the fundamental nature of people has changed through the centuries—I mean, if you read Montaigne's essays for instance, some of his observations are similar. Yet, for all of our time-saving devices, cell-phones, email, etc., how much closer are we to one another and are we using these devices to express our humanity?

Then, of course, there are the cartoons or poorly-drawn characters that would be silly in any age. I know of one doctor at the hospital who literally asked a nurse who purchased a used BMW, "How can you by that car? You are a nurse!" And, this was years before the financial meltdown. The same guy told me that he wanted to live in a gated community because he didn't want the riffraff being able to drive by his house. I told him that I lived in a gated community, too, but that was mainly because I have gates in front of my house. The joke was not appreciated.

Most amusingly, though, was his posturing for medical mission trips. Most of us have done those, sometime anonymously. However, this particular fellow wants to make sure that everyone in the community knows that he is involved. One time, they took a picture in the OR of the surgical team. Everyone was covered with masks, gowns and caps. He literally took off his surgical cap and put on a college cap, took off his mask and stuck his face across the OR drape so that everyone would be sure to get a view of his mug. Then, when the brochures were distributed he took them around the OR, innocently saying, "Have you seen the new pamphlets?" knowing all the while that he was doing it only to show off his picture. You should have heard the nurses talk.

Perhaps for reasons like above, I will always consider medicine to be a trade organization. Certainly, medicine can be practiced humanely and altruistically. But, it is imperative that the doctor bring his life experience and compassion to his trade and this does not accrue to the doctor via his medical training.

One time in the OR, I said to one of the surgical residents, "'Tis a far, far better thing I do than I have ever done before." He looked at me blankly. So, I said, "Beware the Ides of March." I think it was that month. He didn't say anything. Finally, I said, "Give me liberty or give me death." He looked at me and said, "Doctor Boggs, I just don't care about anything outside of my area. All I want to do is operate. That stuff doesn't interest me." Talk about an automaton.

I know that in medical school, maybe for that reason, my roommates were a musicologist, a philosophy grad student and an art history grad student. I would never go so far as to say that academics can't get too specialized in their fields nor be prigs and pedantic, too. However, not being as insulated as medical people can be tends to be somewhat eye-opening for them. Or, let me rephrase. It was for me.

For various reasons—the people with whom I have continued to keep in touch with and remain friends with tend to be my oldest friends or shall we say those of longstanding! Certainly you are at the top of that list. Since you were born a week before me, I still recall how you say that those were the most placid 7 days of your life. Certainly, though, the fix was in because I might have come along but then Sonja entered the picture! I remember being at your house for dinner one night when she had told your father that she had gone out for ice and ended up in Phoenix. She reminds me so much of Cecily!

I still speak weekly with Weagley and Hiser. I suspect that it is the tight bonds that you form as Webelos in Cub scouts! I mean, when you are getting knot-tying badges and working on ant farms, you really are bonded for life. Hiser and I used to tear up the mesa behind his house where he always seemed to have an unending supply of M-80's. We would put them in holes, Coke bottles, pipes. It is amazing that I still have all of my appendages.

Weagley I just saw in San Diego—after years he finally abandoned the Duke City and he is happily ensconced out on the Left Coast with his wife, Steph. I think that he is harder on New Mexico than I am, perhaps because I have been away for so long. It was hard for him to make the break and now that he has, he is just delighted to be in a bigger city, one that has so much more to offer. Meanwhile, when I go back to Albuquerque, I still laugh at the low-riders and how what used to seem like such a big city to me seems so small—if only in contrast to how I imagined it as a child.

Tell me what company thou keepst, and I'll tell thee what thou art.

Miguel de Cervantes (1547-1616)

27 March 2009

> *When I was younger, I could remember anything, whether it had happened or not; but my faculties are decaying now and soon I shall be so I cannot remember any but the things that never happened. It is sad to go to pieces like this but we all have to do it.*
>
> Mark Twain

Dear Dinah,

If I remember correctly, you were mathematics major in college, or if not, at least took a lot of math. Well, my mind is not so much like the random number generators with which you are familiar, but is more like a random thought generator. In medicine we call this flight of ideas, which if severe can lead to several clinical diagnoses. Perhaps I should be careful here or I might end up being committed!

That aside, what burst into my consciousness today was a time in high school, that period when you want to be, "Oh, so cool!" that I went to a record store to get some albums with a friend. I think it must have been Hiser, but I am not sure. Possibly I am blocking the incident. The Rolling Stones album, "Sticky Fingers," had just come out.

It is remarkable to think back on album covers. They were such works of art! I remember pondering over them, staring at them as intended for hours, just savoring all of the little hidden meanings that the artists would put into each one. Elton John's "Goodbye Yellow Brick Road," that wild all aluminum-type one from Grand Funk Railroad, Pink Floyd. Those were as much fun—almost—as the music.

Well, I mentioned in another letter that I can be slightly obtuse—no, that is too generous—really obtuse—when it comes to some things. The "Sticky Finger's," album had the image of some jeans on the front and a zipper. Well, duh! But, no, I didn't pay attention to the image or anything else. I must have been corrupted by McDonalds and secret prizes or such, because I shouted at Hiser across the record store, unzipping and zipping the cover all the while, "What's in here, what's in here? There isn't anything in here!!!" God, it still makes me shudder years later. But, I suppose the saving grace is that I didn't find something in there—that would have really sent me.

I was also thinking about youth versus age since I have been going back to the gym more regularly recently. Going to the gym is a sort of love-hate relationship. I was a real regular, going three times a week and running the other days until I was about 43. Then, I turned into a complete slug. I don't know what happened but I just lost all interest, I didn't get that "endorphin high" from either working out or running. Oh, occasionally I would go and do just a few free weights, but only last for 10 minutes and then get completely bored.

Now, just as abruptly, for the past year I have been enjoying going back. My workouts are good, with stable progress and good outdoor runs. I still consider it to be something akin to knitting needles being placed into my cerebral cortex to have to run on a treadmill—I mean, doesn't that term pretty much describe what it is! But, to get outside and run is again glorious for me.

But, gyms are nothing if not social environments, too. I have been going to the same YMCA for almost 20 years. It is conjoined to a college, sharing the pool—which I don't use, because I seem to have an affinity for the bottom—and the weight room. Therefore, we have a bimodal age distribution. We have the YMCA-types, generally older guys. And, then we get the buff, young and handsome college athletes.

The thing that amuses me and interests me most is that the older guys seem most comfortable in their own skins. Yea for age! There seems to be some sort of camaraderie among the older guys, no competition, sort of like, "ah, you are still here" For the young kids, however, it is quite different. The competition is so strong that they are nervous about everything, themselves, their cohorts and the older guys, too.

For example, I have noticed that if I nod my head or speak to a younger guy whom I have seen but don't know, they freak. Sort of like, "Is that gay?" "What does he mean by that?" "That is really weird!" But, if you do the same thing to a new, "older guy, it doesn't seem to be a problem. Fortunately, over time the college kids get to see you over time and get used to who the regulars are and they gradually settle down. But, the wonderful thing about the experiment is that it gets to be repeated annually. That must be one of the fabulous things about being associated with a college—you get renewed every year. It must be one of the benefits of being a professor.

I know one thing. I wouldn't want to go back to the insecurities that I had when I was younger. One time, in Chicago, I went out bar-hopping with one of my buddies who was always a charmer and did very well with the ladies. Of course, he disappeared immediately after we entered the place. So, there I am, figuring out what to do. Bars were never my natural environment, if you can imagine that. So, finally, I saw two women sitting at the bar, speaking quietly but not in what I would call animated conversation. So, I walked up and asked the one closest to me, "Could I buy you a drink?" The response I got was, "Fuck off, little boy!" Well, that pretty much summarizes my successes in bars.

Realistically, though, I think I was born more of an old man anyway. Some people are athletes, some are "doers." I have always been a reader. I am much more content now with a quieter life. I remember one time one of our friends asked me what I did in the evenings, where I went, what I watched. I said that I read. They were dumbfounded. It was as if people didn't do that. They said, "Isn't that pretty lonely?" So, I said, "No, not really, I read with Paula." So, some people join bowling leagues. Some play in tennis leagues. Paula and I have our reading league!

I guess that gives me an affinity with my favorite fictional character at present, Inspector Kurt Wallander—a Swedish Detective. He is divorced, somewhat lonely, a bit too introspective and perhaps a bit too analytical. He lives in a bleak area, Malmo, of southern Sweden. And, on a daily basis he is faced with the evidence of man's inhumanity to man. But, he also struggles on and emerges—in my mind—as a valiant character. So, why should I turn on the news? Now, that is just too depressing.

How old would you be if you didn't know how old you were?

Satchel Paige

28 March 2009

> *"My girlfriend said to me in bed last night' 'you're a pervert' I said, 'that's a big word for a girl of nine'."*
>
> *Emo Philips*

Dear Dinah,

    For some reason, the story of the British lord being caught en flagrante delicto with the French maid by his wife always amuses me. Upon finding them, his wife shrieks, "Sir, I am surprised!" To which, the unflappable gentleman answers, appropriately enough, "No, Madame, I am surprised, you are astonished." Ah, to have such sange froid.

    But, we always—or, lets I sneak in a royal "we" there—I always think that things like this happen to other people. But, such is not the case. One of our friends, who shall remain anonymous to protect the guilty, was once in a similar situation. His father called and wanted to have lunch with him and he—stupidly answered the phone and begged off, saying, "Sorry, dad, I am busy-busy." So, what did his father do? He trouped across the golf course where this young lad lived and found him and his young wife pleasantly engaged. Dourly, he commented, "Ah, now I see what busy-busy is."

    Personally, I can say that Paula and I have been relatively unscathed by parents and children. Living half a country across from your parents is certainly a benefit in that area. Regarding children, we have only been challenged by Cecily—but of course. In days of old, we used to plop the girls in front of movies on Sunday afternoons and say, "now, you guys watch this absolutely fascinating movie because Mommy and Daddy are going to have special time."

    Well, that worked for a while. But, precocious as she was, I think it only took Cecily until she was five or so to knock on our door—unremittingly I must say—to which I replied, "Cecily, go away, we are having special time." Without missing a beat, Cecily replied, "You aren't having special time. You're having sex." Well, checkmate. That was the end—under that ruse at least—of "special time."

    Perhaps worse was the case of an orthopedic surgeon and his wife who I knew. Their daughter traipsed in on them one time, with an airy comment to the general public at large, "Daddy, where is Mommy's head?"

Ah, if we didn't have them already, perhaps children would be their own best birth control. And, I know looking back on it that my views of them have changed so materially through the years that I am not the same person. I am very pleased and appreciative that God has blessed me with happy, healthy children and permitted them to grow up. I know that when I was younger, I would have considered it absolutely a disaster should Paula and I have had a child with Down's syndrome or some other "imperfection."

It was about a decade ago that my entire opinion on this issue changed, almost instantaneously. I was working in our day surgery unit at the time and there was a little boy with Down's, perhaps five or six years old. He was quite fearful of the procedure—I do not even recall what the procedure was going to be in retrospect, but it must have been something along the order of a tonsillectomy or something not too large. For some reason, he took a shine to me and no one else seemed able to comfort him the same way. He just looked up at me with the most innocent face and said, "Would you give me a hug?"

To this day, my emotions still surge when I think back on that moment. Well, what to do. Of course, I gave him a big hug. And several more. And, took really good care of him. But, then I had to make my way to the men's room and shed a tear. It really brought into focus what a shallow approach I had previously taken in my views of life.

When I was younger, the worst thing to me seemed to me to be naïve or innocent. As I get older, I do not think that being blissfully ignorant of the sadness or tragedies which life has to offer is a goal to shoot for. However, it seems to me that sensitivity, openness and caring are much higher attributes in my constellation of values at present that "being cool," "posturing" and so many of the things that I did when I was younger.

Is this age, wisdom or just being tired and worn-down? I don't know. I would make no claim for the former and I think that compelling arguments could be made for the latter! One of my favorite things is hearing the birds outside of my window in the morning when I get up—they really make a racket. I have "birding" CD's, but just never seem to have taken the time to identify the various species, so I still—at over 50 years of age, just call them, "the birds."

Invariably, on days when I can get up late, Paula will have a pot of coffee ready for me. Then, we sit on the front porch, talking and discussing—what else—the girls, my mom, other stuff—before starting our days. *La dolce fa niente* is a far underrated way of approaching life. I have just been reading "Anthony and Cleopatra" by Shakespeare and it demonstrates—to my mind—the sadness of having dominion over the world like Octavius has. Yes, he is the world's landlord, but Anthony and Cleopatra become immortal. Love, not acquisition and conquest, is the highest attribute.

But, lest I close on too serious a note, I will tell you of an amusing story of when I lived in Chicago. I had a Ford Maverick and the heat had gone out in it—meaning that the defroster didn't work, either. Now, also at this time I was really getting into learning French and to do so would listen to French rock and roll tapes at high volumes. Well, since I couldn't see out of my windshield, I had to wear goggles when I would drive around, with my windows down in the winter. You can imagine the looks that I got, some deranged looking fellow, blaring incomprehensible music with his head out the side of his car in the middle of the Chicago winters. No, there was never any doubt that I could be an Octavius! Dreamer, yes. Living in his own world, yes. Normal by any means. No.

Tomorrow I leave for Mississippi and will continue with my letters. However, I will be "In Search" of a printer, so you might get a quanta of letters at once, depending on my success! Ciao!

If you can speak three languages you're trilingual. If you can speak two languages you're bilingual. If you can speak only one language you're an American.

Author Unknown

29 March 2009

> Written at the Charlotte-Douglas International Airport
>
> *"A jury consists of twelve persons chosen to decide who has the better lawyer."*
>
> *Robert Frost quotes (1874-1963)*

Dear Dinah,

I don't know how it worked out but in January I was called to serve on two different juries. I've lived here for 20 years and not been called and suddenly I am selected for two—what luck! When I was with my former group we used to let people off—we didn't take it out of their vacation time—for the time that they had to spend doing jury duty. And, as president of the group, usually I was left trying to find locums (temporary) coverage for these absences. The group would just suck up the cost. How tragic that I had left the group when I received my summons—I mean, why couldn't it have been on the company dime!

Fortunately, I was able to contact a friend of mine who is a former congressman and also a practicing attorney in town—since I was on the road a lot, I was able to work with the county court and be released from that duty. As it so happens, the case on the court docket for that week was a murder trial. Personally, I would have been fascinated to sit on that jury—if selected—and weigh the evidence. Interestingly, to me at least, is the number of people who told me that they would not want the responsibility for sitting on a murder trial.

Maybe it is because I deal with life and death on a daily basis or perhaps it is because I feel that I could treat the issue with appropriate seriousness and deliberation, but I do not feel scared, inadequate nor overwhelmed by the thought of sitting in judgment on someone accused of such a crime. Actually, I find it of greater concern that we have a large group in our societies who feel that they are incapable of making such judgments.

Realistically, the ability to form judgments, to weight things, seems to me the mark of civilization. If all things are equal, nothing is of value. The word discrimination has really been pilloried. Wrongful discrimination, on the basis of race for example, is obviously reprehensible. Yet, to discriminate, to be a discriminating reader, a discriminating oenophile, a serious art critic all seem to me to be admirable traits and the hallmark of culture. That is probably why I sent you the Magic Flute instead of a compilation of the "Greatest Hits of Snoop Doggy Dog" when I was looking for music to cheer you up. Although, I will admit that some versions of, "The Queen of the Night," can be rather overdrawn.

I was not able to get out of the other jury for which I was selected, though. That was municipal court and I spoke with the woman who does the scheduling and she said that they have a very hard time getting adequate numbers of people to show up for their jury pool. The week I was selected, they called over a hundred people and only 24 people served. Basically, everyone over the age of 65 gets out of it and then there are hundreds of other valid excuses. "My hemorrhoids have flared." So, I did my civic duty and it was really eye-opening.

Municipal court is where cases for minor disturbances are tried—petty theft, trespassing, minor assault. Because of the nature of these charges, the accused are not entitled to legal representation and therefore represent themselves. That in and of itself leads to pretty interesting dramatics. In addition, I found that if they do not show up for their trial, we just can't convict them per se. Rather, the evidence is presented and they are tried in absentia. The outcome might generally be the same, but from a pro forma perspective, it is quite different. No Judge Roy Bean verdicts here: "Bring in the guilty bastard. We'll give him a fair trial, and then we'll hang him."

One of the first trials was a minister in town accused of stealing tires. First, the officers presented their case. Basically, the owner of the tire store noted that he had not authorized this gentleman to remove the tires from the premise. Then, they pointed out that his accomplice had to jump a fence and toss them over to put them in the back of the minister's truck. They emphasized that this area was well off the beaten track and that he had to pull into a remote dead-end area to get to these tires.

The minister's defense was primarily that no one wanted these tires. However, the fence was posted so this blew that argument. Then, he said that he had done it before—which didn't help. Finally, it came out through his own examination that his accomplice who had been tossing tires into his truck, had plead guilty. Needless to say, he was convicted. Divine justice will be later.

Another case was a young man accused of domestic assault. He arrived in the courtroom by himself and sat in the defendant's docket. The accuser arrived and sat at the prosecution table with his sister, who was holding "their" baby. The accused had to present first. Her story was that she went to his house, he invited her in and struck her.

His story was rather truncated, so the real story came out when his sister was called and sworn in by the judge. It appears that the girlfriend called his house and said that she wanted to come by. His sister—knowing he was in bed with another girl at the time, who also happened to be 9 months pregnant with his baby, as was his girlfriend—suggested that would not be a good idea and that "he is always a bear when we wake him up.". However, the girlfriend had called from her car on the street and almost immediately knocked on the door.

Groggily, the boyfriend got up out of bed and the girlfriend at the door (for clarification) entered and started yelling at him. At this point, the other girlfriend emerges from the bedroom—two pregnant girls fighting over the same man—and his sister suggests that the girl from the bedroom make tracks, which she did. Now, the boyfriend keeps yelling at the girlfriend that she should just leave, which she refuses, so he goes out on the porch to get away from her. She pursues him and gets in his face and he pushes away from her and is promptly arrested—because, before coming up to the door, she had called the po-po.

Needless to say, we had a very amusing deliberation in the jury chamber on this case. We most emphatically did not convict him of the charge of domestic violence; we figured that he was pretty much set up by the girlfriend who wanted to get back at him for having another sweet-thing on the side. However, we did think that he most probably was guilty of another charge, not keeping his thingy in his pocket. However, he seemed to be serving time on that already. The judge really read the girlfriend the riot act for wasting the court's time over this case. As a side-note, the entire group left "en famillie."

On a sadder note, we had two people who showed up late for their trial and the judge—who was meticulously fair, I must say—asked them why they were late. The woman said that they didn't have an alarm clock. The judge really looked askance at them over this, but when he asked them where they lived, they said that their families had kicked them out and they were living in a tent. Apparently, they were living in an abandoned house which his family owned—with no heat, and you have to remember this was February and we had snow. When his family found out that he had HIV they were all afraid that he would infect them (by osmosis, I guess) and they told them that they had to leave the property. We in the jury pool were so uniformly sad and depressed over this—and then we discovered the charge. Trespassing, for being on his family's property. He burst into tears and asked not to be sent to jail. I think we were all delighted when the judge asked him if he could work a couple days at the dog pound and he suspended his wife's sentence.

One last story comes to mind. There was a young couple, attractive in a very rough way, sort of a la Bonnie and Clyde types—but, with a strong uneducated and country emphasis if you can picture that. Yeah, I know—hard to do. They were up on charges for an altercation—fighting with a very pretty female officer on our force (I didn't know we had any—it must be hard on her because I can imagine the jokes. Will you handcuff me?)

Anyway, in the first go, the prosecutors—the police really—accepted everyone randomly from our limited pool of 24 potential jurors. After being accepted by the police/prosecutors, however, you had to be accepted by the defendants. However, this young guy thought that he would do psychic profiles on each potential juror. Therefore, a former bank president got up and he declined him. Another well-dress white woman got up and he struck her. Finally, I was called and walked up. You could have heard him through the courtroom. "Not him!" he intoned.

I suspect that he thought that if he got sympathetic black females on his jury panel he thought that he and his girlfriend would be OK. Maybe he figured that blacks have had problems with the police. However, maybe he didn't read the chapter on the fact that they don't like crime more than most of us do, either. Maybe he should have read another chapter, with both his girlfriend and him being white. But, their minds are places I would not want to go alone. Needless to say, my friends, black and female, on the jury pool sent him to jail. We chuckled about that in our "deliberations" on break.

Well, tomorrow I start early at the hospital in Mississippi—so fun to spell, I hope the work proves so too!!! I have more jury stories but will save them for a later day.

"Only Lawyers and mental defectives are automatically exempt for jury duty."

George Bernard Shaw (1856-1950)

30 March 2009

> *I want a new drug*
> *One that won't make me sick*
> *One that wont make me crash my car*
> *Or make me feel three feet thick*

Huey Lewis, 1983

Dear Dinah,

I was drinking tea—cold, iced and most definitely in my case not sweet-tea!—at "The Delta Grind" tonight when I got your voice mail. Yes, I am in Mississippi. And, uneducated as I am, I have to inquire tomorrow about where this "Delta" stuff comes from. I am "Up-State" and I really always thought of deltas as being down near the coast. I have so much to learn.

Regarding the tea, you may not know it but sweet tea—like kudzu—is a Southern tradition. I thought that Carter would absolutely go apoplectic when she got to UVA which is far enough north to be cultured according to some, to not be gentrified according to others, and they had no sweet tea. The chagrin! She told me, "Daddy, you are just going to have to rent a tanker trailer and send me some." Perhaps the one time I haven't complied with one of her requests.

Sweet tea in the south is made so toxically sweet that you do not need to worry about bacterial growth. The osmotic pressure from all of the sugar molecules is toxic to all forms of life, save blond women and men in camouflage. It reminds me of a boy Carter dated who nearly laid me on the floor laughing over a comment he made. We passed a bunch of guys in camouflage, lounging near one of the watering holes at UVA. So Joe said that he would like to run over them and say, "Oh, I am sooo sorry—I just didn't see you!" Well, needless to say, I am seeing more than my fill of camo down here in the Delta.

A propos of the letters, I wanted to tell you that I was delighted to receive your voice mail tonight. I am sorry that I missed you but exceptionally happy that the letters are brightening your day. I really love mail—the entire family teases me about it because it usually is bills, anyway. Nonetheless, I love the sound of the drop in the slot. Moreover, a letter, versus even a call or an email, can be read over and over, savored and enjoyed. That is why I thought they would be the perfect tonic for you. However, doctor's advice—this is my treat to you. Please, you are under no obligation to write or respond—just lay back and hopefully enjoy!!!

Tonight I was thinking about a special story which I have never shared with you—I am going to save some of my travel stories for later in the week. Rather, I do not know if you know how I "earned" my first—and shall I say my last—fraternity election.

To begin with, let me say that I was never a "pot-head," but like our former and current president, I have indulged and was a "child of the 70's." However, let me say that alcohol would always have been a preference for me because pot made me sleepy. I have been called at various times in the past, "coma man," because I would fall asleep when others were just cranking up. Ah, now, I do love my sleep!

In addition, pot had other bad effects on me. One was that whenever I smoked it I seemed to find a body of water and dive to the bottom. I truly cannot tell you how this was processed in my mind—if you can imagine that. Do you think it was growing up in arid New Mexico? Suffice it to say, on more than one occasion at parties friends would have to scoop me out of the deep end. "Oh, oh! There goes Boggs again. Who is going to dive in and get him this time?"

Well, on my notable night, I was just a new member of Sigma Chi. We were going to have a big house party for the entire campus. We had a three floor house, with a band on the first floor and lodging on the second and third levels. For the party, we made the girls' bathroom the second floor bathroom and the men's' the third floor bathroom. The kegs were in the basement. We did have one brother we had to watch like a hawk, because he was notorious for hanging on the fire escape outside of the girls' bathroom and try to catch glimpses of them engaged in natural functions. However, that is just creepy and is purely incidental to my story.

On the night in question, doing as well with the ladies as I usually did in college—which is to say, not well—I proceeded to have several beers . . . . well, a few more than that if truth be told, in the basement. It was a spring night and the weather was beautiful and the air was lively. The music started cranking—again, remember, this was before techno and all that other stuff, but we still played it loud. LOUD. The house itself was vibrating.

So, I amble around the house and see people dancing but that was not for me. I wander up to the second floor to one of my buddy's rooms and he is smoking some weed and purely from a polite and socially obligated perspective I feel that I wouldn't want him to do that alone. So, we muse and zone out, feeling the music. The band was right below his room so the entire floor was shaking.

Now, if pot made me sleepy, pot on top of alcohol always had another effect on me—it made me nauseous. So, I try to deal with this as well as I can by sleeping a bit, quite unsuccessfully I might add. Poor choice of locale. I chose a bed right over the band. Talk about shaking and baking.

Suddenly, it was as if I had been resurrected from the dead. Overwhelming nausea just hit me and I could not control it. So, what is a guy to do? Obviously, I ran down the hall to the bathroom.

Minor problem. The hall had a line stretching well-back from the bathroom with attractive young co-eds. Blond, brunette, red-haired—I am sure they were all there. However, that was most decidedly not my problem. I had a mission and I did get into the bathroom. Yes, there was a lot of screaming but I—fortunately in my state—did not hear it. I raced to the sink and misguidedly aiming up vomited all over the mirror. Needless to say, the girls fled. Several of my bigger brothers were summoned to take care of the disturbance upstairs, but it took quite a while for even them to pry my hands away from the sink. I do not remember where I spent the rest of the night, but did wake up back in my bed. Alone.

I truly dreaded the next day, Sunday, having to go eat in the dorm dining room. But, I needed some coffee. So, I wandered down the path to the common area and passed a pretty girl. She asked, very nicely, "Are you feeling OK?" I nodded affirmatively. I passed several more and in each case, I received more solicitations for my welfare than I had received all year.

Later that night, we had our house election for fraternity officers. I was nominated for treasurer and after my performance the preceding night was under no delusion that I would be considered. So, we did this office and that office, the nominees sequentially filing out for the discussion and vote. Finally, the office of treasurer came up, the one for which I had been nominated. Several of us left the chamber of secrets. We sat quietly on benches, looking at each other. Then, there were loud voices from inside the meeting room, indistinct at first, then growing more animated and audible. Finally, one voice shut the others up and said, "Anybody who can party like that deserves to be our treasurer." We were called in after the vote, but I suspect that reasoning is how I attained my first and only fraternity office.

"I wish I could drink like a lady

I can take one or two at the most
Three and I'm under the table
Four and I'm under the host"

Dorothy Parker (1893-1967)

31 March 2009

> "Hard to believe that one night more than sixty years ago, during a dance that had turned rowdy, someone hit Lawrence Welk over the head with a brick in Hague, North Dakota."
>
> Ian Frazier

Dear Dinah,

By now you have some stories from my side of the family. I thought you might like to hear about some of Paula's relatives. Surprisingly, my dark-haired beauty is of Scandinavian descent—that certainly goes with the name, "Johnson," intoned with a lilt like something out of Fargo. Paula's father was born on a farm in North Dakota and I am sure that I will get the story mixed up, but basically times were really hard during the depression, so when the parents died Paul (Paula's father—do you think he wanted a boy?) and one brother stayed on the farm to work it. Another brother went to Annapolis and became a naval officer and the last of the four, a girl, went to live with wealthy relatives.

One of the saddest things that Paula has told me about was reading some of her father's diaries, about the loneliness of growing up, being responsible for a working farm at his age. I mean, it is not the type of abusive depravation that we read about in our newspapers now, with children chained in basements and forced to do horrible things. However, the maturity that he and his brother Leyland had to assume at such a young age meant that they did not have the jocular and jovial adolescence that we think accrues to youth in our era.

Paul was—if nothing else—a very studious and attentive student and through diligence was able to get into Temple medical school in Philadelphia. It was in Philly that he met Paula's mother, Penny. Penny—like me, was adopted. And, my birth mother was adopted, too. So, I guess the only thing that runs in my veins is adoption. Or, possibly, the inability to delay gratification!

I do not know the specifics, but now my interest is piqued. However, I do know that when Paul saw Penny he fell desperately, impossibly in love and the feeling was mutual. Years later, when Paula's father died, her mother confided to her that he was more than a husband to her, but had been also like a father and a brother to her. Despite this impossible love,

Penny probably did go along with Paul's move to the Cleveland Clinic to do his orthopedic residency, but I believe that she probably did question her love when he proposed taking her back to North Dakota.

Obviously, during this period, Paul had to serve in the Medical Corp and children came along—I do not know the exact details, save for the fact that Paula was born in Philly, then came Dawn, then Greg and finally Jill. The entire kit and caboodle ended up in a big, roomy house in Bismarck, which Paula remembers to this day. Paula also remembers lying out on the plains in N.D., looking in wonderment at the summer sky, marveling at the number—incalculable—of stars in the sky. She also remembers how in the summer, the water in the swimming pool where she took swimming lessons was absolutely freezing—especially for a tall, lean lanky girl.

Growing up, Greg must have been the handful. One time, caught stealing, his mother sent him back to the drugstore with the item "in hand." Following his apology to the owner and the item's return, she asked him if he learned his lesson. "Most definitely," he said. Seeking further assurance, she inquired as to what the lesson was. "Well, I'm not shopping there anymore! They know me." Would it surprise that Greg is a practicing attorney?

Greg also traumatized Paula's younger sister Jill, whenever he could. For years, at the dinner table, he would chant a slight tune, under his breath. Jill would burst into tears. Finally, determined to get to the bottom of this, Penny made Jill spill the beans. Apparently, Greg had—for some time—convinced Jill that she was born a black baby. Through a magic known only to children—mainly Jill and Greg—she had turned white, but when her black mother would come to reclaim her, she would be singing Jill's special tune, "Oong-Ga-Boog-Ga-Chow-Wow, Take my Child Away!"

It would be unfair not to portray Greg as loving, which he certainly was. They have a cousin, Paul (I guess those Swedes ran out of names) who has some land on a river near Bismarck. In the summers, he told me he used to see a tent down by the river and he would stop his horse in the mornings and Greg would emerge, followed by an attractive young woman. A week or two later he would ride the same way and he would pause his horse, Greg would emerge from the tent, followed by a different attractive young woman. This would go on for entire summers.

Speaking of Paul, he—in his own right—is a remarkable character. Rarely have I met someone so genuinely nice. We went to a wedding in Charlotte, N.C. in the middle of summer. Everyone was dressed in seersucker or khaki as befits good Southerners and were dying in the heat and there was Paul, in a black shirt and black jeans. And, black cowboy boots. He walks with bow-legs from riding all of his life. I started talking to him, asking him about what he does. He told me that he got out of cattle ranching because his doctor told him it was too hard on his back.

I must go back a bit and say that everything with Paul begins very slowly and is said as, "Well, Steve." Then, the comment will begin. "You see, the Doctor told me that I had to stop with them cattle. They were killing my back." Now, take how long it took for you to read that and multiply it by about 20 and you might have a flavor for Paul. So, needless to say, we had a long talk. But, he astounded me.

"Paul, what do you do now?"

"Well, Steve, I like those sheep"

"Paul, why is that, Paul?"

"Well, Steve, those sheep are just so much smaller than those cattle."

"Paul, how much do cattle weigh?"

"Well, Steve, those cattle weight about 2 tons, and those sheep, well they just weigh about 200 pounds. I just pick them up and set them where I want them."

You can see why Paul impresses me. Here is this guy, out arranging sheep in a field all day—primarily because cattle got to be too heavy! One time, when I get the chance, I am going to take Paul up on his offer to take me shooting out in N.D. I can't think of a nicer person to spend time with.

There are so many other stories that I have learned through the years. However, for today I will leave you with one special one. Dr. Paul was always working—being the only orthopedic surgeon for a 4 state area in those days. So, Penny and another friend, George Wright, who worked on the paper, would come up with plans for amusing themselves. Jill had a date whom she was very interested in, some "cute guy" who she had been hoping would call. As luck would have it, he did ask her out. As luck further had it, Penny and George had other ideas.

When the hapless "dat-ee" appeared at the door, Penny appeared with a double-barrel shotgun—I do not know how she was dressed. All she said was, "Are your intentions toward my daughter honorable?" That was the last that they saw of him!

"Winnipeg is like Fargo, North Dakota, without the action"

Billy Jay

1 April 2009

> *"You do not know how much they mean to me, my friends, and how, how rare and strange it is, to find in a life composed so much of odds and ends . . . to find a friend who has these qualities, who has, and gives those qualities upon which friendship lives. How much it means that I say this to you—without these friendships—life, what cauchemar!"*
>
> T.S. Eliot

Dear Dinah,

    Happy April Fool's Day! I had given some thought to what I could do for a special letter for today, something light and frivolous. However, events have conspired against me so I feel more like writing something a bit more serious, despite the occasion.

    I think that the real tipper in my emotions concerning topics was a text message that I received this morning when I was working in the OR. Apparently, our neighbor who lives across the street and was 96 passed away last night. Libby had suffered from multiple lingering illnesses and this can be viewed as a release of her suffering. However, she will be sorely missed.

    When we moved to Gaffney almost 20 years ago, the first morning that we work up in our "new house," our present house, we looked out on the porch and there were some freshly baked biscuits and a pot of coffee. Energetic at that time, when she must have been in her 70's, Libby was always very active well into her 90's. Several years ago, her family finally took away her car privileges from her. Since I had to do the same thing with mom, I understand—in retrospect—their fear of her reaction. They took her out to lunch and her brother took her car away and sold it. It was gone when they returned.

    For several days she did not speak to them—literally. For years, she did not forgive them. It must have been one or two years after they did this that I went to sit and drink some coffee with her on her porch. Jokingly, I treaded where I should not have gone. I said something about driving and she gave me a deep, penetrating look in my eyes. She said, "they stole my car." Libby had a good sense of humor, so I really didn't know how to take this. So, I said, trying to keep it light, "well, you know, they will take you wherever you want to go." She looked at me and said, "Steven, you know in the Bible that it says that you should forgive your enemies. Well, I just don't think that it applies in this case." And, this was her family. I might note here, too, that Mom told me that she was driven to church by Libby one night and didn't think that she would survive the experience. Libby liked to go straight down the middle of the road, other cars be damned.

Libby was from a very old-fashioned, Southern family with the values that you do not hear about in the media too often. They had blacks working on their land, but her Daddy and his workers all did the same work. And, there was no racism in the family. Libby said that it was not anything that was a topic of discussion—she just knew that certain words or behaviors were intolerable to her parents.

This would have to be contrasted to the behavior of another Southern woman in our neighborhood. This lady lived in a very large house, not a small condo, as did Libby. She had been a school teacher and her husband "acquired the house" during the depression. She always used to say, "He always had an eye for distressed properties," with a wonderful Southern drawl. In point of fact, when you live in town a little longer, you hear rumors that he had robbed the bank during the depression and did several years in prison. The money was never found. Who knows what the truth was. But, it made a great story.

This lady was also, like Libby, sharp as a tack even in her advanced age. After her 95th birthday, Cecily made the comment, "She only has 5 more years left." Actually, that was correct, but probably not prescient. Rather, I believe that Cecily couldn't conceive anyone living past 100—there must be a rule. She always plead poor vision, but she could really see things at a mile. You would constantly be amazed when she would come out with things like, "Oh, I love those flowers that you planted in (the very distant) corner of your yard." And, she read the cover of the local paper cover to cover daily.

Yet, Mrs. Etang was not an inherently kind woman as was Libby. Her son was killed in an automobile accident during WWII (not combat related) and she truly never recovered from the loss. However, she used to be incredibly cruel to her daughter who was devoted to her and came to see her daily. She would make cutting comments, even alluding to how, "too bad it wasn't you." Such behavior just defied belief.

Moreover, she was racist to her bones. A woman who used to cook for us when the girls were in high school—because if you didn't know it, Paula absolutely hates cooking, but that is a totally different letter!—had an aunt who used to work for Mrs. Etang. In fact, we got Etta after her death. (Mr.

Etang had died years before). This aunt was cleaning Mrs. Etang's kitchen with a mop when Mrs. Etang came in and told her to scrub the floor better. The absolute nature of the argument is lost in the mists of time, but when Mrs. Etang insisted that this lady get down on her hands and feet and clean the floor by hand, and when she refused, Mrs. Etang started kicking her. Then and there, Etta's aunt left the house and left Gaffney and went to NYC.

When we moved south, from Philly and D.C., our friends in the northeast looked at us as if we were crazy. Personally, I think they could have envisioned us moving to Angola or Sierra Leon before Gaffney. When we told our neighbors in D.C. that we found the people very welcoming, the guy said, "Well, that's just 'cause you're white and you're rich." Well, I can't argue with the former assessment and I know the second is not the case. But, I must say that even Mrs. Etang did have absolutely fascinating stories.

One afternoon, I sat with her and she told me about her relatives—I think to get it right, it would be French, the DeCampagnes—who lived in New Orleans. I do not remember all of the details now but I heard all about how her grandfather had died in a yellow fever epidemic in New Orleans in the 1850's. They were just piling the bodies on carts and throwing them in places with lime to help prevent decay. I heard this story on her sun porch under the oldest world map that I had ever seen—even then.

One thing that I love about the south, in addition to the climate, is the living, breathing sense of history. Our house was on the Christmas tour as a fund raiser for the garden club this year. The president of the garden club told me that his grandfather fought in the Civil War. I corrected him and said, "No, you must mean your great-grandfather." He said, "No, I mean my grandfather." I said, "You have got to give me the dates for this."

His grandfather was born in 1840 or so and fought in the civil war, or as they call it here, the war of Northern aggression. Most Southerners don't get completely into this, but there are a few diehards whom you do not want to engage on this discussion. I know when we started looking for houses down here people said, this is a nice, older house, built before the war. Well, you and I coming from Albuquerque—I only know about one war and I thought, "These houses look much older than that." I guess you have figured out what took me some time—they were talking about "Mr. Lincoln's War," *The War*.

But, I digress. After fighting in the war of state's rights, his grandfather got out, worked, and then ended up marrying his grandmother around 1905, when his father was conceived. His grandfather died when his father was young, but his father lived a long life and married late in life also.

Therefore, this fellow—who is now only in his 60's—is not that old for having a grandfather who truly fought in the civil war.

I have taken quite a path away from my good friend Libby, whom I trust is liberated from her suffering at this point. She had suffered several strokes in the past few years. Moreover, she had—and I lose count—something like 3 knee replacements on each knee and also bilateral hip replacements and revisions. And, until just recently she kept walking. I encouraged Mom to keep visiting her as an inspiration, because Libby was just never one to give up. I will not be able to back out of my driveway without thinking of her.

I deliberated whether to write this in a letter—I mean, do you put this in a letter to a good friend recovering from surgery. However, your voice mail said that you are getting stronger. So, I thought, first, Libby's life was a testament to never giving up. Second, she exemplified grace and presence in advancing years—and, you and I are only one—half her age, so I hope we can use her as inspiration. Finally, she made me think of my favorite meditation. I have cited parts of this at times in eulogies which I have had to deliver for friends. I think that Donne beautifully shows how we are all so closely interlinked, you, me, Etta, Libby and the Mrs. Etangs' of the world. I am thankful for every day which I have been given, sitting here in the sunshine writing this letter to you. So, let me close by appending the entire text which I love so much for you—hopefully—to reflect upon. Trusting and hoping that you are stronger every day!

Meditation XVII by John Donne

PERCHANCE he for whom this bell tolls may be so ill, as that he knows not it tolls for him; and perchance I may think myself so much better than I am, as that they who are about me, and see my state, may have caused it to toll for me, and I know not that. The church is Catholic, universal, so are all her actions; all that she does belongs to all. When she baptizes a child, that action concerns me; for that child is thereby connected to that body which is my head too, and ingrafted into that body whereof I am a member. And when she buries a man, that action concerns me: all mankind is of one author, and is one volume; when one man dies, one chapter is not torn out of the book, but translated into a better language; and every chapter must be so translated; God employs several translators; some pieces are translated by age, some by sickness, some by war, some by justice; but God's hand is in every translation, and his hand shall bind up all our scattered leaves again for that library where every book shall lie open to one another. As therefore the bell that rings to a sermon calls not upon the preacher only, but upon the congregation to come, so this bell calls us all; but how much more me, who am brought so near the door by this sickness. There was a contention as far as a suit (in which both piety and dignity, religion and estimation, were mingled), which of the religious orders should ring to prayers first in the morning; and it was determined, that they should ring first that rose earliest. If we understand aright the dignity of this bell that tolls for our evening prayer, we would be glad to make it ours by rising early, in that application, that it might be ours as well as his, whose indeed it is. The bell doth toll for him that thinks it doth; and though it intermit again, yet from that minute that that occasion wrought upon him, he is united to God. Who casts not up his eye to the sun when it rises? but who takes off his eye from a comet when that breaks out? Who bends not his ear to any bell which upon any occasion rings? but who can remove it from that bell which is passing a piece of himself out of this world? No man is an island, entire of itself; every man is a piece of the continent, a part of the main. If a clod be washed away by the sea, Europe is the less, as well as if a promontory were, as well as if a manor of thy friend's or of thine own were: any man's death diminishes me, because I am involved in mankind, and therefore never send to know for whom the bells tolls; it tolls for thee. Neither can we call this a begging of misery, or a borrowing of misery, as though we were not miserable enough of ourselves, but must fetch in more from the next house, in taking upon us the misery of our neighbours. Truly it were an excusable covetousness if we did, for affliction is a treasure, and scarce any man hath enough of it. No man hath affliction enough that is not matured and ripened by and made fit for God by that affliction. If a man carry treasure in bullion, or in a wedge of gold, and have none coined into current money, his treasure will not defray him as he travels. Tribulation is treasure in the nature of it, but it is not current money in the use of it, except we get nearer and nearer our home, heaven, by it. Another man may be sick too, and sick to death, and this affliction may lie in his bowels, as gold in a mine, and be of no use to him; but this bell, that tells me of his affliction, digs out and applies that gold to me: if by this consideration of another's danger I take mine own into contemplation, and so secure myself, by making my recourse to my God, who is our only security.

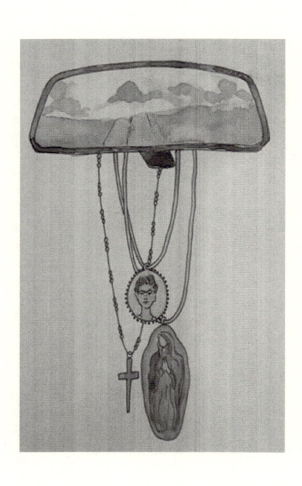

2 April 2009

> *A single tree in the tropical forest in the south of Mexico has more different species than some European countries.*
>
> Carlos Salinas de Gortari

Dear Dinah,

After yesterdays serious letter, I thought that we would go traveling again—to one of my absolutely favorite destinations in the world. It has received such bad press lately, what with the escalation of crime due to drugs and illegal immigration. I am sure that in the wrong places those are issues of major concern. However, I also remember that when I lived in Washington, D.C. it was the murder capital of the U.S. But, if you were not involved in drugs and stayed away from areas infested with drug sales, your chances of being killed were actually quite low—that was back in the 80's. So, I intentionally ignore all of the "evidence" we are presented with against going to Mexico and instead tell you why I am enchanted with the place.

First, I must say that I must be positively biased in favor of "the other." One of my partners teases me because I told her that I do not like to vacation anywhere they speak my language. I just don't feel that I have been away if I hear English where I go. Maybe that explains my Franco versus Anglophilia. Likewise, when I took my job in Pennsylvania, I came back and was telling the women—who incidentally happens to be black—who takes care of Mom that I didn't know what I would do—there just didn't seem to be any black people in Pennsylvania where I am moving! After living in the South for 20 years, this will just be too much of a shock.

In a similar vein, maybe it was our growing up in New Mexico that has affected me, but I am very distressed by the gross ignorance of most American's about our own history. I know that one night on OB I was speaking with one of my partners. He was complaining about having to do free care for illegal immigrants. Now, I don't even want to wade into those waters because I do believe in border enforcement and that a nation should regulate it territories. However, once people are here I feel that we have pretty much an obligation to care for them without complaint and when you get right down to it, this poor girl is just a pawn in the system. These are systemic problems, not things that are her fault.

Therefore, I couldn't help but play devil's advocate. I said, "Well, realistically, since we stole roughly half of Mexico's territory in an illegal and fabricated war, perhaps these people are just coming back to reclaim their territory." He looked at me blankly and then said, "You don't know what you are talking about. We've never done anything like that. We are America." Therefore, I had to explain the entire background of the Mexican-American War to him and point out that Polk had just been looking for a causus belli—which the Texas issue among other things—permitted him to declare war and invade Mexico.

The Treaty of Guadalupe Hidalgo just crowned our basic theft of this land. But, in that era, there was enough guilt to go around. The Mexican government was weak and ineffectual. But even Abraham Lincoln thought that war wrong and demanded to know "where the spot was" where American blood had been shed.

But, this is not the fun stuff. Where to go in Mexico? I have been to some places in the Yucatan, to San Miguel de Allende and also to Mexico City. Today, I want to write about Mexico City. All of what I have written before was to clarify that I am not completely insane. But, on my 50th birthday, I thought to myself, self I thought, how can you consider yourself a "cosmopolitan guy" if you have never been to the biggest city in the world? So, despite all of the objections of friends, who thought it was insane to plan to spend your 50th birthday in "a big, dirty city," I cashed in all of my frequent flyer miles and booked 8 days in Mexico City with Paula.

Now, I love to travel but am not cavalier. So, I knew not to take taxis off the street, get them from the hotels, etc. And, unfortunately, since we were cashing in frequent flier miles, we were in a business hotel—not ideal, but luxurious. Not the way to know the city best, though. So, I had arranged a shuttle to pick us up at the airport when we arrived. Needless to say, after we "de-planed"—what a term!—we went through customs and then were ambling through the land transportation area. Where was our sign with our name on it?

Suffice it to say, some guy said, I have a cab and against every natural instinct, I said, "OK." Well, he didn't just take us to a cab stand. We ended walking, pulling our luggage through side streets next to the airport, through a chain link fence. Then, we get to his "cab," which is being very generous. Basically, it was his low-rider. But, the carpet on the dash was actually a very attractive hue and I did like his statue of the Virgin Guadalupe. I just hoped that my death would be swift and that they would be gentle to Paula.

Despite this, we did arrive safely at our hotel—late in the evening and it turned out to be beautiful, right in the downtown area of the Paseo de la Reforma, we ended up at the Marquis Reforma. Personally, I am not used to traveling like I work for AIG so it was a treat. The rooms were great. Usually, Paula and I pry ourselves into some tiny Parisian room and end up stacking our suitcases on top of themselves. So, attentive service and luxury was wonderful. But, admittedly, it is not the way that I like to "mix it up" with the natives.

The next day, we spent the afternoon in San Angel and Coyoacán, which are wonderful market areas—with funky alternative places to amble. However, what I loved more was when we went to the Frieda Kahlo museum. I had seen the movie, "Frieda" with Selma Hayek and looked over some of her art before we went to Mexico. She did a wonderful interpretation, even getting Frieda's fearsome unibrow look going. Also, I knew a little about her tortured relationship with Diego Rivera. But, the soul and inspiration of her art—taken in context of the personal physical and emotional tragedies of her life, her broken back(s) and heart, they just are heartrending.

My favorite work is entitled, "Broken Column." It shows Frieda with her chest and body open, a piece of metal supporting her neck and back. The power of this work really resonates with me. Then, being able to walk where she lived—and at times, Diego did, too—and see her studio, her paint brushes, and courtyard—it is a journey to Mecca for someone who is drawn to her work. Certainly, her work is not to all tastes, but I find her to be one of the artists—of all types—who speaks to my soul.

Near her house is the house where Leon Trotsky lived when he escaped Stalin and fled to Mexico—I might add, unsuccessfully—to live and write. He had a compound and I mean a compound. There were high walls with gun turrets and wire around it and a guarded entrance into the area. There were chicken coops where he cared for some hens and his office, family living areas, a large garden.

Unsurprisingly, though, he was murdered by an NKVD agent sent by Stalin who gained his trust and thereby entrance to his compound, house and office. He stabbed him in the head with an ice pick! Creepily, there is a list of all of the early Bolsheviks and what happened to each of them in a museum on the premises. In every single case, Stalin was able to successfully secure their murder.

Well, this is just the first day in Mexico and I have so much more to tell! I guess that will wait for the next day or so.

"My driving abilities from Mexico have helped me get through Hollywood."

Salma Hayek

3 April 2009

"Woe to the man whose heart has not learned while young to hope, to love—and to put its trust in life."

Joseph Conrad

Dear Dinah,

I haven't forgotten that we have to finish our trips to Mexico City and even more distantly, Istanbul. I will get there. Yet, like my mother who never can tell a story without a bunch of interesting errata, I will give you some other (hopefully amusing) errata along our path. It is like I always try to emphasize to the girls—the path is more important than the goal!

Today I was going to tell you some Chicago stories, first of all about how Paula and I met. At that time, I had finished my first quarter in my third year of medical school. Internal medicine was one of the more demanding rotations and I had just finished that rotation, which included general medicine and some heme-onco and some cardiology for me.

Several of us planned to go down to Rush St. do let off some steam, but when push came to shove, it came down to just me and another buddy—Mitch—heading up along LSD (Lake Shore Drive) from the South Side to North Side to party the night away. Mitch and I wandered into various bars and finally settled on one which seemed to be throbbing better than the others.

On walking in, looking around and generally getting a lay of the land, Mitch said to me, "Look at that beautiful woman over there. I'm going to talk to her." Well, Mitch was correct in once sense. Over near the fake bowling machine was a tall, angular brunette, extremely attractive, with shorts on, white socks on and penny loafers. I though that she was gorgeous. I also saw that she was talking to someone else—a guy. "You can't go talk to her—she's with that guy." "I don't care," he responded and headed over that way.

Mitch started talking to the duo, obviously focusing on the girl, and I tagged along. I was astounded. The girl—who was Paula—seemed pleased to speak to him and kept talking with him. On the other hand, the guy wasn't quite so happy—he looked rather irritated, didn't say anything directly, but was—as we guys say, "Pissed." Not knowing what my function was in this group, I served as a pseudo-Gunga Din, bringing beer for everyone.

Well, we talked for a long time and Paula who was smoking at the time looked like she needed another cigarette. So, one of us offered her one. This other fellow really took offense at this. "Yes, go ahead, let Mitch and Steve give you beer and cigarettes! Just feel free!" And, she did. And, he—stupidly in my estimation—stormed off.

The plot gets more complicated here as I learned in retrospect. Paula had come to this bar, "The Lodge," with her ex-husband and this guy had run into them. They had had some drinks and Paula couldn't get rid of this guy. After her ex left, this guy kept hanging onto her, even though she was out for a night of fun. So, in point of fact, she would have been pleased to talk to Quasimodo to get rid of this guy. Enter, Mitch and Steve. And, I thought that it was our sparkling personalities. And, beer and cigarettes.

So, as beers and time passed, Paula does that thing that women do when the want to dance. She started doing something with her shoulders and moving a bit in time to the music—you have to remember that although the fashions were atrocious in the mid-80's, we did have good music. And, I sort of deferred to Mitch, who had gotten us this far. But, he did nothing but talk. Finally, after about my "n-th" sortie to the bar, I said to Paula, "Would you like to dance?" She said, "Sure," so we went to the dance floor in the lodge which gives a postage stamp a good run for economy of use of space. But, if nothing else, a gentleman should show a lady a good time. And, despite the fact that I would rather have a root canal than dance, I was adequately lubricated at the time and with a beautiful woman, so I had few complaints myself.

While we were dancing, I asked Paula if I could have her phone number and if I could call her again. She scrawled it down on one of the cocktail napkins from the bar (we still have it in one of our photo albums—at least I do; the best cocktail napkin I ever received). Going back to talk to Mitch, we talked a bit more, but then we decided to move on and Paula wanted to "stay and play" longer.

When we left "The Lodge," I excitedly told Mitch, "I got her number!" He said to me, "Give it to me, too!" I said, "Are you out of your mind—she will really think we are a couple of trolls if we both call her. And, I asked her for it and I'm not giving it to you." It would be a gross simplification to suggest that the conversation ended there, but I held my ground. Perhaps it was Kismet, perhaps it was fate. Perhaps, it was my recollection of my other experiences in Chicago bar. But, I—Steve Boggs—really, really, really—got a phone number from a live and pretty woman in a Chicago bar. I was not going to share that gold medal with anyone.

The next morning, I remember waking up really early, something like 8 AM. Cell phones weren't big in those days, so I got out my napkin and called Paula. Excitedly, I said, "Hi, Paula, this is Steve! I wanted to see if you want to go out to dinner next weekend?" Even more dramatically, I remember her first—possibly non-intoxicated—words to me. "Steve who?" Quelle horreur!

Nonetheless, I was not put off and we did work out arrangements to get together for dinner, although I do not believe that it was at that particular phone call. I remember the anticipation that I had for our big, first date. I was truly an impoverished medical student and had little money and I knew that Paula was working downtown in Chicago. Yet, I was not about to let this deter me. I broke into my piggy bank. Literally. I had something that I stuck all my change into and had been doing so for a couple of years in Chicago. I opened that sucker up and counted out every penny, nickel, dime and quarter and got something like $80, which was sufficient in those days.

I investigated and called some romantic restaurant downtown in Chicago, an Italian restaurant where you could look out and see them giving carriage rides. I specifically told them that I wanted a nice table for a special evening. I picked Paula up and we got to the restaurant and Paula disappeared into the ladies. They escorted me to some horrible table, back near the rest rooms and by the bus boys' station. So, I was presented with a quandary and had to figure this one out.

Looking around, I saw that there was only one table like I really wanted, looking over the carriages, by the window. Glaring back at me was a little, elegant sign in the middle, "Reserved." I neatly solved that problem. I walked over, sat down, and pocketed the sign (paper). Paula emerged, I waved her over and we had the first of many memorable dinners. The rest, as they say, is history.

"Who ever loved that loved not at first sight?"

Christopher Marlowe

4 April 2009

> *"Our houses are such unwieldy property that we are often imprisoned rather than housed by them."*
>
> *Henry David Thoreau*

Dear Dinah,

When we moved to Gaffney, we looked at several houses. Our house—which we ultimately decided to buy—was a spooky looking red brick house with little to commend itself from the outside when we first glanced at it. What sold it to me, though, was when we walked in the main hall and there were 10-foot high pocket doors. Perhaps it is the romantic in me. Maybe I had seen too many 30's and 40's movies, but pocket doors for me—a boy who had grown up in Albuquerque, just were so evocative of an elegant style of living that I had never experienced. Paula knew then and there that this would be our house.

However, you do not move into an older house in the South and have it become yours. Yes, on paper the title may transfer to you—or, in my case, the bank may be the owner and I may be a nominal renter. But, the house will always be referred to as, in our case, "Mary Griffin's house."

Mary Griffin was a doyen of our itty-bitty town. I am totally positive that I will get some of the facts wrong, for which I would be pilloried by those with full knowledge. But, on the other hand, should I not make a stab at this, you never receive tutorials in these important things.

For an outsider, you gain local knowledge slowly, have to sort of come at it indirectly, like a Poirotian detective, accumulating the facts and history of the people who have lived and live in your town. This is not the case for the locals. I believe that it is concatenated into their DNA, giving them unbelievable processing power for the most intricate social networks.

"Yeah, you remember Billy Bob? He was Suzie Parker's boyfriend in high school before she started dating Dewayne. Well, anyway, he and a couple of other good 'ole boys were up at the lake with Deborah and Sweetback when this big 'ole cottonmouth come up and bit Onion—who was there with Tammy—and they were sort of messin' 'bout a bit, 'cause she and her 'old man have been having problems. Well, it bit Onion . . . you get the idea.

Returning to Mary Griffin and the facts which I am sure that I will screw up, she was the daughter of a wealthy man in town. Our house and the house next to it were "companion houses," and shared a circular drive between them, years ago. Our house was the baby house and the neighboring house was the more spectacular of the two. It had the porte cochere and the fine parquet detailing on the floors inside. Mrs. Griffin was the daughter of the guy who lived next door.

Her husband worked for American Brands Tobacco, but realistically it appears that he was more along the lines of early CIA. He used to spend long periods of time in Turkey and was a personal friend of Ataturk. Mary would take the family with him sometimes. One time, after they returned to our house in the winter, they found that they couldn't open the front door. Apparently, a pipe had burst and ice covered the first two rooms. So, taking the opportunity, they took all the furniture out and had a skating party in the rooms, before they had to have the flooring replaced. That is why we have heart of pine floors in all of our rooms, save for our most elegant rooms. There we have oak.

We bought the house from Gaylord Perry, a famous baseball player. He used to coach at Limestone College in Gaffney. Gaylord, fortunately, had done the basic plumbing and other things. However, when we did look the house over, it still had—in parallel to the new wiring—the old, exposed wire DC current wiring from years ago, wrapped around ceramic turns. In fact, under the stairs, there was an archaic light bulb made with a human hair. Unfortunately, that bulb was gone when we took occupancy.

Other treats were servants' bells in the walls and also in the floor and an ice window for ice deliveries. And, what touched me the most was in the carriage house one day I found these stickers of airplanes. They had been applied by the little boy, George Griffin, when he played there during WWII. There must be about 10 of them stuck to the rafters. I muse on the hours of amusement that he must have spent, fantasizing about being a pilot. I must find a way to preserve them.

When we remodeled our bathrooms, which originally had the delightful but not really comfortable claw-footed tubs, I also found this weird apparatus in the attic. I didn't know what it was, it was about two feet tall, cylindrical, with pipes coming out of it. Dewayne, who does work for me, said, "You don't know what that is, doc? That's a still." I forget that our house needed one during prohibition. It reminds me of one of my elderly patients who told me one day, "Son, you forget, I'm old enough to remember when alcohol was illegal and pot was legal." Q.E.D.

I say all of this about our house to say that it has become a part of our life, not because we paid so much for it! I think we bought it for something like $160,000 when we moved down here years ago. I truly wish that I had spent no more than that on it, not the case. But, it has been a labor of love and we truly feel as if we have salvaged a valuable part of our town's history.

I would suggest that—should you ever be so inclined—that you not remodel three bathrooms at the same time, especially when you live with teenage daughters. Because we tore out all of the bathrooms, all of us were compelled to share a postage stamp area of a makeshift shower, toilet and sink. Once, seizing my single opportunity to shower with some degree of privacy, I carpe momentum-ed into the bathroom, jumped into the shower and was covered in luxuriant hot water. Suddenly, I heard all of this motion in the bathroom and there was Cecily (noted, by peaking around the curtain). Totally exasperated, I said, "Cecily, can't you just give me a few minutes alone?" Without missing a beat, she said, "Oh, take your shower. I don't want to see that little thing of yours, anyway."

However, I must say that I did try to give as well as get. One time, Carter—at that most difficult age, when parents are just sooo inconvenient and embarrassing—came back from Victoria Secret with some new underwear. She was so proud. I don't know what got into me, but I put a pair of her panties on my head which really got her going, chasing me around the house. Who would have known that the UPS driver would ring the doorbell at the time. Of course, from my perspective, I have told you how I love mail and a package proved to be even more interesting. So, I completely forgot about the panties and answered the door. Fortunately, the driver knew me and with a totally straight face, just handed me my package. It wasn't until later that I realized how I must have looked. Fortunately, social services were not called.

> *"I do not want my house to be walled in on all sides and my windows to be stuffed. I want the cultures of all the lands to be blown about my house as freely as possible. But I refuse to be blown off my feet by any."*
>
> *Mahatma Gandhi*

5 April 2009

> *"Friends are like television. Some are like PBS and always asking for money. Others are like the news, with sad tales to tell everyday, some are like that one station with the foreign language; you don't understand a word of it but you listen and watch."*
>
> *Unknown*

Dear Dinah,

I know that we were talking on the phone about the girls speaking other languages—Carter, French and German and Cecily, French, German and some Japanese. I think—as I alluded to in a previous letter—that your mother might have had something to do with that, because I was always so impressed with the ability to speak other languages. So, from early on, I resolved that I—a monolinguist—would do everything that I could do to make sure that they would learn to speak more than one language.

I think it started in Washington. I still get unmitigated grief, from both the girls and Paula, over my approach to "language learning." What I did at that time was to put a lock on the television so that the only stations the girls could get would be the Spanish channels. I figured that they would migrate to Spanish cartoons. This only proves how wrong one man can be. But, it had other indirect benefits. The girls never watched television and instead became very focused on playing outside.

My next gambit was to have them watch Muzzy, a BBC language program. It has a toxically nauseating theme song which makes Paula still recoil to this day. I had no idea how imprinted this was on them until I was speaking to Carter the other day. She was giving me chapter and verse about "the Princess" and "the evil guy" and "the peaches." It did come back to me, but this stuff really imprinted into her. And, into Paula because when I mentioned it, Paula knew about all of these things. But, as for Spanish learning, it didn't really do much here.

When we moved to South Carolina, I bought this program called "French in Action." I loved this show, in large part because it was easy and fun. And, perhaps more significantly, it had a beautiful heroine, Mireille, who could speak French to me for hours. She could be saying, "This is blue and you are green," and I would be transported—on a cloud of fantasy—to Paris, enraptured and in love with the entire French experience.

Sadly, I wrote to the programs creator, Pierre Capretz at Yale and asked him for advice on how to teach the girls French at a young age. I never got a letter back. I am sure that he though, "Mais, who issss deees imbecile daan deeer?"

For the girls, my next approach was to discover the Concordia language villages in Minnesota. That is a really professional program for kids, well-taught. So, one summer—at the earliest age possible—we shipped the girls off to Lac du Bois or something like that! I don't remember much from those summers—no anecdotes wended their way to me.

However, as the girls got older, I decided that they should experience *la vrais France*. I don't know where I come up with these things, but I found a camp in the Pyrenees for the girls. Paula was nervous about the girls being on a different continent, so far from parents. So, I solved that *tout suite*. I enrolled Paula at The University of Perpignan for the summer.

The stories from those summers are wilder. The one that I know most distinctly is about Cecily. Apparently, her group went hiking all day and then decided to go swimming. Cecily's shoes ended up floating into the middle of the lake and the counselor—who liked her—had to feign protest—go retrieve them for her. This became for the summer the story of "Cecily and the story of her amazing shoes."

Paula, in contrast, complained bitterly about being away. I am like thinking, "Duh, you are in France, I am on call." But, Paula was thinking, "Paris it ain't." She went through the local museum in about 2 hours and unlike me—who would probably know everyone in town by the time I left—spent a lot of time reading and studied really hard. However, she was in a dorm which was not air conditioned. She did like her fellow students, but felt very homesick. This was not an experience to be repeated. In addition, the nurses at the hospital told me that I was a bit randy, like a March hair, by the end of the summer, so they too were glad that this would not be an annual plan. I mean, I don't think that I was rubbing up against people's legs like a dog at a cocktail party, but I must have really missed Paula.

Fortunately, by the following year, the girls were old enough—most definitely in Paula's estimation!—to go to France by themselves. I researched and found that the accent near Tours was supposed to be very pure for French. So, I found a place for them to study for the summer and subsequently, the girls spent three summers in Tours. If by nothing else but serendipity this proved to be an inspired choice. The city was large enough to hold the girls' interest for this period of time, yet was also small enough to be accessible and safe for them to get around in.

Cecily had a boyfriend each summer in Tours. The first summer, she also met a kid there from Seattle who has remained one of her best friends. He really liked Cecily and told her that she was under no circumstances to get a boyfriend the second year until he got to France. Unfortunately, he was too slow, arriving one or two days late the following summer. This is pretty much Cecily's window of opportunity for boys, and by the time he arrived, she already had a new boyfriend. The last summer they were to go to Tours, he planned to get there before her and was all set to preempt any opposition/competition. However, circumstances conspired against him—I believe his plane was delayed—and again he arrived one or two days late. Once again, Cecily had a new beau. I truly think that Carter found this the funniest thing that she had ever heard of when she found out what happened.

Before college, the final year of studying overseas was then I sent the girls to a more "professional" language school in Montreal called Point 3. The girls really loved Montreal. They ended up starting there when the Formula 1 racers were there (I don't think that they go to Montreal anymore). Needless to say, they became fast friends—no pun intended—with several of the mechanics and other people involved in the race. Heady stuff for young girls from Gaffney, S.C., where going to "Little Moo Dairy Barn" is the big thing to do on a Saturday night.

It was just when they were really getting into the school and also the swing of Montreal, going out each night, really loving life, that we received Paula's diagnosis of breast cancer. That was almost 5 years ago now. Paula was so stunned that she didn't even think that they would come back to be with her. Perhaps, since it was not my diagnosis, I think it took me about 2 minutes to figure out that the girls were coming home. Their mother needed them. The school was exceptionally gracious and helpful in coordinating things for us and right away, the girls were home.

Skipping over that summer, which constitutes a totally different letter, after that the girls decided that they needed to expand into German. So, they spent summers at the Goethe Institute in Munich and also Freiberg studying German. I think it might be the fact that they had studied French since they were little or just that it was something new, but Carter in particular really loved German. She said that it seemed to work more the way her brain worked. I mean, German is very organized and logical whereas French is . . . . well, so French!

"In general, living in a foreign country has been amazing. To experience a new culture, attempt to learn a new language, try new foods. It's something I'll always be grateful for."

Sue Bird

6 April 2009

> *"Delivery" is the wrong word to describe the childbearing process. Delivery is: "Here's your pizza. Takes 30 minutes or less."*
>
> *Jeff Stilson.*

Dear Dinah,

I don't know that I have ever told you the stories about when the girls were born. Carter was born when I was a resident in Philly. Paula was in great shape, since we had just moved from Chicago where she was a workout fiend. Every morning she would get up and do the treadmill for a long time. Music was not ubiquitous then, as now, with iPods and everything else, but she did have an Walkman. However, she only had a few tapes. I believe that Carter is the net result of many a turn on the treadmill to the Eroica Symphony.

Paula wanted to do everything perfectly with Carter, although to be honest, we did not know that it would be a "Carter" at that time. Everywhere we went, people all would ask to touch her stomach. Taxi drivers, doormen, people in stores. Everyone, everywhere told us without exception that because of this or that or the lay of the dog in the alley that we were going to have a son.

Well, wanting to do everything just right with Carter meant that Paula ate well and didn't have any ciggies and eliminated alcohol from her diet. And, she really didn't gain much weight. She was not like some of the women I see at the hospital who view pregnancy as carte blanche to gorge themselves for 9 months. I mean, if you have a 7 pound baby and some placenta and some water, should you really gain 60-100 pounds? Don't think so, but perhaps I am a food Nazi.

Nonetheless, by the end of her pregnancy, thin Paula was sick and tired of being pregnant. She wanted that baby out. And, she wanted a drink. Finally, when our sweet little bundle had not made its appearance, we had a dinner planned with my relatives, Robert and Melinda. We went to a great restaurant and had a lovely meal and Paula had two glasses of wine. I am sure that she would be convicted of some crime under today's more fascistic regimens, but it seems that this proved to be the tonic.

The next morning, my last day of work before vacation—which had been very iffily timed to begin with, trying to be off to help out based contingently on delivery time! In those days, there was no such thing as paternal leave. Yet, at 5 AM, Paula started having significant contractions. Her water broke—I might have been more help to her if I had grown up on a farm, since I was still rather helpless. It took me a while to process that this was her water breaking and that we were going to have a baby. Duh.

Collecting our "little bag," we went downstairs and our doorman opened the door for us. Since I didn't have a car at this point, we had to flag a cab. I flagged one and he pulled over, looked at Paula, shook his head and drove off as quickly as he could. Paula looked at me and said, "Get me a cab!" Our doorman saved the day. He said, "Let me handle this. I will get the cab. Once I get it, you get in—indicating me—then, after you are in, Mrs. Boggs can follow."

This worked like magic. We got some sort of Nigerian guy who didn't know what he was in for, but didn't know how to get out of it either. We lived on Walnut St., right across from the University Hospital, but that meant driving over a bridge with metal supports. Every second, the cab would bounce up and down, especially since he was driving like a maniac, probably for fear that the baby would come in his cab. With each bounce, Paula would give out a little shriek of pain.

We were deposited, most unglamorously, at the hospital. Taken to her room in OB, the obstetrician assessed Paula and told her that she was a "9" and that it could be 30 minutes or a few hours. He offered her an epidural, but suggested that she didn't need it at her stage. Ignoring him, she informed him that it would be placed.

While this was going on, some of my fellow residents wandered in, not to see Paula but to check on me and to tell me about some of the latest parties, news and other sundry items. We were all happily engaged in conversation, chattering away when Paula gave me a dirty look and said, "Get them out of here while I am in pain!" However, shortly thereafter, the beast was tamed by Brett Gutsche, an OB guru. Paula has forgotten her obstetrician but still remembers Brett fondly.

Carter was delivered 4 hours after the first contraction. Conveniently. During daylight. With no sleepless nights for her parents. Paula, by virtue of her epidural, actually ended up visiting by phone with her sisters and friends, episode concluded happily. In marked contrast, was Cecily. Cecily was delivered while I was on active duty in Washington and she made her entrance at Bethesda Naval Hospital. Strangely, military regulation and order are the furthest things that come to mind when I think of Cecily.

Paula and I had just settled into bed, about 11 PM, when Paula went into contractions with Cecily. This time she was going much faster. Driving really quickly through the back roads to the hospital, Paula was admitted to the unit. However, the guy—a friend of mine—who was supposed to come in and do Paula's epidural rolled over and went back to sleep. By the time he would have been called in again, Cecily was "born-ed" to use the word that she used for years.

So, Paula received Stadol. It was supposed to "take the edge off," according to the nurses. Paula hated it. She said that it just made you drunk when you were pain free and didn't do a thing when you were hurting. Fortunately, Cecily was delivered around 1:30 AM, so Paula didn't hurt for that long a period of time.

Yet, using only birth time, projecting forward you could anticipate that Cecily would prove to be the more trying baby—which indeed was the case. From about 3 months of age, Carter would go to bed around 8 PM and sleep undisturbed until 7 the next day. Her hours were very regular. Cecily in contrast, was nocturnal, Ms. Par-tay. She wanted to sleep all day and then, would wake up around 7 PM and want to be entertained all night.

She had an uncanny knack for knowing when you were not attending to her. We had a mechanical swing which would work for about 30 minutes. But, then, she would figure out that you were getting comfortable or engaged in something else and she would scream her bloody head off until you would pick her up and walk her around. Paula was so frantic that she called me at work on day out at Andrews AFB and said, "You are putting Carter in day care." I didn't want to spend the money—which we didn't have at the time. However, I knew by the tone in her voice that it was either we figure something out or else I might be receiving a military funeral. Would that qualify for Arlington?

It turned out that between Carter playing all day and then Cecily wanting to be up all night, Paula was at the edge. Fortunately, the woman across from us there ran a day care and—I have no knowledge of the arrangements or what Paula did to get Carter in mid-year—but quick as you say, Tom Cruise really messed up on Post-Partum depression, Carter was gone all day and Paula became one really happy camper.

"It sometimes happens, even in the best of families, that a baby is born. This is not necessarily cause for alarm. The important thing is to keep your wits about you and borrow some money."

Elinor Goulding Smith

Palm Sunday, 2009

Written after services at St. James Episcopal Church, Greenville, Mississippi

"Church: A place in which gentlemen who have never been to Heaven brag about it to people who will never get there"

Henry Louis Mencken

Dear Dinah,

Writing these letters to you has made me realize one thing about my life in particular, how uniquely blessed I have been. I know that that is a very old-fashioned sounding word to hear nowadays. I have read Sam Harris' and Richard Dawkin's books on atheism and understand the philosophical arguments against faith. Rationally, much of what they say makes sense.

However, it reminds me of the anecdote of the rabbi who has to adjudicate a dispute between two in his congregation (I don't know if that is the right word, but I use it in lieu of not knowing the correct one). Anyway, the first person very passionately presents his side of the argument, listing all of the reasons why his side should prevail. The rabbi nods attentively and says, "You're right." The next person get up and likewise presents a very logical and compelling rational for why, in actuality, his side should prevail in this argument. With deep understanding, the rabbi furrows his brow, nods and says, "You're right." The rabbi's wife looks at him like he is insane and says, "They can't both be right!" He looks at her and replies, "You're right."

That is somewhat where I am in my faith-path at present. For years I was an agnostic, which in my case meant that I was not ready to do the heavy lifting or actually take a position regarding faith. It was much easier for me to slide aimlessly along, saying, "Well, nothing can be proven."

I think some of my major spiritual influences are both Thomas Merton and Buddhist literature. I remember reading "The Seven Story Mountain" and literally feeling as if the ground had been knocked out from under me. I believe that it was a little too big "C" catholic for Paula, but I absolutely felt that Merton was speaking to my soul. Here was a well-educated, thoughtful, intelligent man who seemed to look at the world from some of the same angles which I had seen it from.

Likewise, I have found great solace and inspiration in Buddhist readings. Cosmic unity, dealing with suffering, detachment—yet, not implying disinterest—all seem to promote a health way of living in harmony in our world. I believe that we in the west discount the vast spiritual knowledge and literature of the east at our own loss.

I know that probably somewhere in this body of work I should cite the bible as my primary inspiration. However, while it forms the corpus for my beliefs, I think that being an Anglo-Catholic as I am, I view it as a work of history, literature and other elements, not as the Muslims do their Koran and the fundamentalists do, the literal word of God. After so many translations from the Aramaic, Greek, Hebrew, I just cannot believe in biblical inerrancy.

No one less than the Dali Lama said that you should pursue your faith tradition in the stream where you find yourself. I don't know if that is an exact quote, but he said something like that that I read. So, what is a poor boy in Gaffney, S.C. to do? I find myself at home in the Episcopal Church. One thing that struck me in my reading of Thomas Merton was when he said that he and a bunch of Buddhist monks got together—they had no problems communicating. However, when some of the non-contemplative orders got together, they just couldn't understand each other—they were so concerned with theology and legalistic approaches to religion.

I am not discounting theology, but my emphasis in my life is Christian community. My mother—back in the day—and I had disagreements over this. She would watch T.V. evangelists and consider herself a Christian. It is not for me to say, but I do not believe that Christianity can be practiced in isolation. I believe that it is a communal religion. I know that when we have had family problems, such as Paula's illness, our faith community was essential.

Furthermore, as I age, I find the statistical arguments either for or against God's existence to be less and less of interest to me. O.K, I know there are a lot of stars, and the chance of life out here is such and such. Likewise, the philosophical/logical arguments and all the rest are fun to play with, but they really do not work on me. I think that I have to come down on Tertullian's side, with credo quia absurdum. However, people so frequently do not understand this. Tertullian had an ironic wit and could not escape from a good phrase. Yet, his basic argument was that what I believe in cannot be proven. That is where my faith comes in.

Perhaps I am soft but what I find to be compelling is the look in the eyes of another person. I don't care whether I am treating them, working with them or just placing an order in a fast food restaurant. The spark of humanity that I see in others is what makes me a believer. I know this can be practiced as a Buddhist, Muslim, Hindu or other faith, but I chose to practice it as a Christian. There may be many ways to approach the godhead, but you do have to choose one. Vacillation does not lead to enlightenment.

One thing I will say about the Baptists is that they know their bible, better than I ever could learn it at this late date. But, maybe it is better to know just a few things well. I do know that in both the Old and New Testaments the Great Commandment is "To love thy neighbor as thyself." I also know that perhaps the finest suggestion on how we should live—individually and as a society—is the Sermon on the Mount. Even a Marxist friend of mine is inspired by it. I, particularly, love the Beatitudes:

And seeing the multitudes, He went up on a mountain, and when He was seated His disciples came to Him. Then He opened His mouth and taught them, saying:

> "Blessed are the poor in spirit,
> For theirs is the kingdom of heaven.
> Blessed are those who mourn,
> For they shall be comforted.
> Blessed are the meek,
> For they shall inherit the earth.
> Blessed are those who hunger and thirst for righteousness,
> For they shall be filled.
> Blessed are the merciful,
> For they shall obtain mercy.
> Blessed are the pure in heart,
> For they shall see God.
> Blessed are the peacemakers,
> For they shall be called sons of God.
> Blessed are those who are persecuted for righteousness' sake,
> For theirs is the kingdom of heaven.
> "Blessed are you when they revile and persecute you, and say all kinds of evil against you falsely for My sake.
> Rejoice and be exceedingly glad, for great is your reward in heaven, for so they persecuted the prophets who were before you.

8 April 2009

> *"My generation, faced as it grew with a choice between religious belief and existential despair, chose marijuana. Now we are in our Cabernet stage."*
>
> *Peggy Noonan*

Dear Dinah,

I'm not sure that I've ever told you about one of my first girlfriends at college. I know for sure that I didn't tell my parents about her. It was over the summer—I was taking summer school and I was living in the frat house. St. Louis in the summer, without air-conditioning, with a bunch of guys, is a truly disgusting experience. It was hot. As Robin Williams said in "Good Morning, Vietnam," it was crotch pot cooking hot. I had two fans blowing over my bunk, one blowing over me from the feet and the other blowing away from me at the head and it was still really hot. As a kindness, I won't even describe the bathrooms for you.

Living in such close quarters, there were bound to be—shall we say—disagreements, among highly hormonal youths, or as my New York brothers would have said, "Yutes." I know the reputation that women all cycle together. I do not know what the physiological phenomenon for males is, but there is definitely something there—basically they all get pissed off together. Usually, however, it was related to foosball in those days. I do not know what would be the precipitant now.

We all shared the kitchen, which again—in that long list of places that you really would not want to go, that would be one of them. Community appliances with all of the associated headaches and charges. We had one brother who was very moralistic, a good Christian man, who resented any implication that he was a food thief—even though everyone knew that he was the culprit. This was coupled with the fact that he was very vocal over the fact that he had never, ever and would by no means ever would smoke pot.

What to do? Well, some of the more—shall we say, Baconian brothers, in honor of those who respect the scientific method—decided that there was one very quick and sure way to evaluate the hypothesis. "Does Brother X steal food?" Several of them got together and baked a tremendous batch—and I underestimate by saying tremendous, since it was a magnificent, amply, wonderful and bodacious batch—of pot brownies. The only remarkable thing about this experiment was that they were willing to chance being wrong—that Brother X might not be the culprit—and risk their pot. It shows the degree of general consternation over his behavior and also the vast quantities of food which he had been removing from the Serengeti.

Task completed, all that remained was to put the brownies out and wait. And, it did not that long before said brownies were gobbled up. However, it did take a little while for the effects to be manifest and what would they be? Within about 2 hours, great commotion was heard in Brother X's room. Slamming of drawers, moving of closets. This was not really the effect than anyone had anticipated. With trepidation, one by one we slinked into his room and he had thrown all of his clothes out of his third floor window to the lawn. Why? No one ever knew. He was in tears, explaining something that none of us could understand. But, he did it in a very loquacious manner.

He had eaten the entire pan of brownies and was super-stoned. And, when he came down, he was very angry—still denying that he had eaten anyone's food. And, like the lawyer who says, I am innocent, but if I had done it, you couldn't prove it, he went on to get very angry over the fact that anyone in the house would dare try an experiment like that in our community.

This all was meant to serve as context for my summer digs. So, we had a party one Friday night and—typically, I must add—I attended stag. Many of the brothers had dates. One of my brothers brought a very attractive date, a short, cute brunette. I must have been feeling my oats that night because I waited him out. The three of us were talking and finally he said to her, "Would you like a beer?" She nodded and I made my move. "While he is getting you a beer, would you like to see the roof?" She nodded and I couldn't believe my luck. It was like fishing if you aren't prepared. What do you do if your bobber starts going up and down?

Knowing only one thing to do, I took her up to the third floor, where my room was, and made some very lame excuse and said, "Hey, come in here and see this first!" So, we went into my room and to be discrete, I shall only say that the lights dimed (but they didn't), the door locked (and that it did, because my brother was bigger than me) and a good time was had by all—save for my brother who pounded at the door for a while but finally gave up.

As it turned out, we had a great deal in common. I was a studious engineering and pre-med student. And this girl worked alphabetizing the phonebook in St. Louis from Aaaa to Aaaz. At that age, thought, it was sufficient common interest because talking was about as far from anything that we were doing as possible, in fact, it might have been a distraction.

One day, though, my Polish lover—whose name was very heavy on consonants and quite short on vowels—invited me over to "meet the rents." That was fine with me. What really freaked me out, though, was when she started going through her hope chest. First, I had never seen nor heard of a hope chest. Second, some of the stuff was just cheesy. Now, I certainly came from a middle class background at very best but the thought that my life would be determined by this hope chest made me retract like a rubber band pulled maximally.

The last I heard—because, like all good guys, I still called "just so we could spend an evening together," but she was smart enough to stop that—was that my former girl had abandoned me for a guy who was the assistant manager of a McDonalds. And, looking back on it, if you amortize it over the 30 some odd years since then, if he stayed with McDonalds, he probably came out to be a much wealthier man than I.

However, my sweetie did leave me with much than only pleasant memories. After our parting, I remember—naive me—having this absolutely burning pain "down there." It was horrible. I washed and scrubbed and did what I could to no avail. At the point of desperation, I finally went to student health, a place no sensible student wanted to appear in those days.

I signed in and the girl behind the glass said, "What is your problem?" I said, "I will tell the doctor." She repeated her question twice and then finally, not receiving satisfaction, called out, "Bessie, would you take this student to Room A?" So, I was led down some long, echoic hall with tile floor and amplifying walls. Getting me to my room, closest to the waiting room, Bessie said, "You have to tell me what is wrong." I didn't know what to do—I didn't know what it was. So, I dropped trou and showed her. Her face lit up, she literally shook with laughter and she shouted out in those reverberating halls, "White boy's got the crabs!" I asked to leave by the rear entrance.

> *"Crabbed age and youth cannot live together;*
> *Youth is full of pleasance, age full of care;*
> *Youth like the summer morn, age like winter weather;*
> *Youth like summer brave, age like winter bare"*
>
> *William Shakespeare*

11 April 2009

> *"Each of us is meant to have a character all our own, to be what no other can exactly be, and do what no other can exactly do."*
>
> *William Ellery Channing*

Dear Dinah,

Up to now I have tried to avoid mentioning any medical stories. However, after speaking with you on the phone I feel sure that you are making great progress. In addition to that, medicine has been such a major part of my life that it is pretty hard to leave that part of my life out of some stories. So, I will share with you some these vignettes, some pretty amusing, some quite sad.

When I was a medical student, I started my ward medicine rotations on general medicine and also on hematology/oncology. In those days—and, I am not saying this is not the case now, just that it is so far out of my present purview that I don't know about the department—the hematology section at Chicago was phenomenal. They had specialists on diseases with wonderful names like "Hairy Cell Leukemia" and "Von Willebrand's Disease."

Three of us started as eager "rotators" on I-3, the name of the heme/onco ward that summer. And, as luck would have it, that was when I ended up meeting one of my first patients who I still remember to this day. Sandy G. was then a young girl in her early 20's from a Polish Chicago family. They were a wonderful family and extremely caring. Needless to say, they were all terrified over the diagnosis of leukemia which their daughter had received and had come to the medical Mecca for treatment.

I was responsible for all of the blood drawing and rapidly became a vampire, as do all young medical students in inner city hospitals where students do the "scut" work instead of paid blood teams. I would get in early, check her labs, receive direction from my resident (which, since this was my first rotation involved pretty much in telling me to do everything and how to do everything). We would assemble everything for rounding with the attending. Depending on who your attending was, you might either have a great rotation or might die presenting (or not) at the bedside. "Boggs, what is the incidence of acute lymphoblastic leukemia in this age group?" Suddenly, the fire escape would look quite inviting.

We would progress from room to room on I-3, the medical student presenting to his level of ignorance, then the intern would fill in. The resident would then offer some insightful words of wisdom and the fellow would reflect that in some very obscure journal it was recently noted that a new regimen of Cis/Boom/Bam was used successfully in the Pima Indians in the treatment of a combination of diabetes and ALL. The attending might—or might now—add content. Depended on his or her mood. Then, the entire entourage would migrate, like a plague of locusts that had decimated one field and were looking for another, to the next patient's room. The medical student would receive encrypted directions—get abdominal CT scan, new LP, serum porcelain level.

I became very close with Sandy G. and her family over the course of that summer. I mean, you do not repeatedly go in every morning, deal with the expectant faces of the family, present the news that you have—understanding that you are not the final word—while keeping the major information for your superiors to release as they saw fit. Sometimes in the evenings, I would go by just to talk with Sandy. Perhaps it was her age and I am sure that a psychologist would see self-identification there. I am sure that it was. Certainly, it was just easier to go and spend a little time talking with Sandy than some ancient—as I see it now—40 or 50 year old patient. One problem with medicine is that you have to start so young, since the path is so long. By definition you are immature when you begin.

I remember when I found out that Sandy died. I was not on her service and might have even been on an away rotation. However, it was as if a spike had been driven through my heart. I had not personally lost many people in my life up to that point and here was this young, vibrant woman who I had recently spoken with, spent time with—and she was gone. I cannot tell you how profoundly this affected me; I suspect the fact that I can still see her and remember her name—now almost 30 years later—is sufficient proof of that fact.

If Sandy was the thread which coursed through my medical student year, Linda H. was the cord which grabbed me as an intern. Although I planned to do anesthesia, I wanted to stay in Chicago and do internal medicine for my internship. That tells you how old I am—we used to separate internship from residency. Moreover, I felt that internal medicine would best prepare me for anesthesia since anesthesia involves so much medicine. My surmise was not totally incorrect.

As luck would have it, I ended up starting my medical internship on—you guessed it—I-3. And, my first patient was Linda H. If I had grown to be very close with Sandy and her family, Linda really was an experience. She was a beautiful, blond, amazingly sweet and gentle soul. She must have been no more than 18 at the time and again from a very close Polish family. She, too, carried the diagnosis of leukemia.

By this time, I was much better at blood drawing so when the medical student couldn't get things I could help. We were a very busy service and internship year is not a year for spending time with patients. However, I do remember occasionally when I was on call checking in on Linda and her family, just speaking to see how they were. Things looked good. She had a very good response to her induction chemo.

I ended up wending my way through GI, cardiology and various other rotations. Occasionally, going through I-3, I would see Linda and her family. As the year went on, things got worse and worse. Each time I would see them, I would spend a little time, try to comfort them as I could—quite ineffectually I am sure—but do my best.

Finally, I have forgotten the rotation that I was on but it was toward the end of my internship. Someone must have know that I had become close to the entire family because they told me that Linda was in the ICU and was extremely critical. I went up to the unit and she was literally about to expire. Which she did. Her family was in the waiting room next door and I could have just left, but I couldn't. I went in and her mother was in tears. Her father was angry. He was saying, "I should never have put her through this. This has been horrible. All of this and I lost my girl."

I know that the ideal is medical detachment but I certainly did not have any that day. I just burst into tears and cried and cried with the family. There was nothing to say. I felt so sad for Linda and for her family. And, if truth be told, for myself. The amount of love this family had was self-evident and there was no justice in their loss.

After that day, no patient has effected me in quite the same way. Many have come close. But, my heart was torn in a certain way that day and it has never been the same. I know that something in me died that day, too. Yet, importantly, I have tried never to get so hard that I couldn't shed some tears for a patient.

"If I'm going to sing like someone else, then I don't need to sing at all."

Billie Holiday

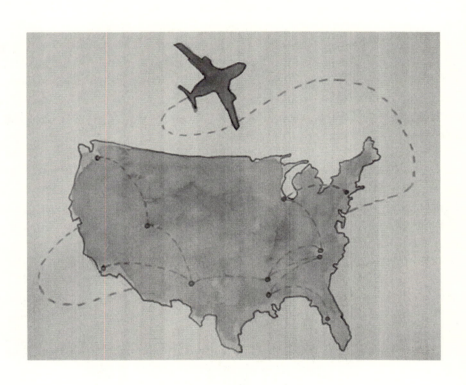

12 April 2009

> *"Home is where one starts from."*
>
> T. S. Eliot

Dear Dinah,

    I never really liked our "better" house on Spring Avenue, compared to the first house I knew and grew up in on California Street in Albuquerque. In the early 60's, California was so convenient. You could easily ride your bike to the 7-11 (in those days, parents had no concerns about kids doing things like that!). I remember that summers, in particular, were magical because all the kids in the neighborhood would ride their bikes around the street until after dusk. I loved that because I got the first "banana seat" on the street, so I truly was very entitled.

    Thinking back on it now, we really were a herd of young boys in the neighborhood. All of the parents must have come back from WWII and just gone at it like bunnies to have had such cohorts like that. Despite occasional arguments, really there were no major problems. But, why is it that there always has to be "the tattle tale" in the neighborhood?

    We had one and his name was Brad. I remember distinctly one afternoon one of the kids on the street wanted a new bicycle but knew he would never get one—his folks didn't have the money. So, we put our heads together and I agreed to repaint his current bike—that would be the next best thing.

    The decision was to do this project in the middle of our driveway—which had no oil spots on it, which made my father very proud. It was clean, virgin concrete. What, though, does a young boy of 5 know about such important issues? We plopped the bike down in the middle of the drive and I must have pulled out 6 or 7 cans of paint from the garage. I had seen my Dad do this million of times on other things, so I was a pro.

    We were a large group of boys by this time—say 5 or 6—and the painting was going well. Frame. Spokes. Tires. I was fairly indiscriminate in the coverage—only in the sense of not being selective concerning what I was painting. I am sure that I was quite generous in terms of quantities. This all was going on while my mother was chatting and drinking coffee in the picture window looking out over the drive. There was obviously tacit approval. Who would have thought that adults could become enrapt in conversation?

But, if it had been a melodrama the key would have switched to minor because Brad came up the drive with that infuriating, all-knowing, "I-am-going-to-ruin-this-fun" type manner. "You shouldn't be doing that." Everyone ignored him. "You're making a mess on your daddy's driveway. You shouldn't be doing that." Still, the group stuck together. "That bike looks really ugly!" (Brad, you should have seen it before.) However, there was a little murmur of anxiety in the ranks. Finally, "I'm going to tell."

Well, this was just insufferable and intolerable. There was only one way to handle this. Walking over to him, I took the paint can and sprayed Brad. Covered—before he ran away, because I see now with my knowledge of neurophysiology that it took his neurons a few microseconds to process from eye to leg that he should get his butt out of there—by my trusty can of paint. Draw, partner.

That did eliminate Brad for a short time but did not prove to be a long-term solution. Unfortunately, very shortly thereafter Brad—can you be a painted child?; I have heard of painted women—and his mother came past me and shuffled up to the front door. My mother was then presented with a litany of my evident—and self-evident—guilt. Worst of all—Brad, whose parents were as poor as church mice—had just bought his first new pair of pants since his birth. This doubled the insult. So, after suitable punishment which I do not recall, my parents replaced Brad's pants. Bike was painted. I should drive by the house on California next time I am in Albuquerque to see if the stain in the drive is still there.

Perhaps a little worse than that incident was the time that I heard that an older man on our street had recently had a heart attack. We were all counseled to behave and "not disturb him." I didn't know what a heart attack was but I wanted to see the effects should he be disturbed. So, one night he was driving slowly up the street and I ran in front of his car. He slammed on the brakes, got out and said, "I ought to spank you for doing that!" I replied, "You do and my parents will sue you!"

I ran home, not being totally stupid, and acted so innocent in the kitchen. "It smells so good in here mom!" The phone rang. I ran to pick it up. "No, you have a wrong number." Click. The phone rang again. "No, same wrong number." Click. Finally, when it rang the third time, my mother got there before me and said, "I will get it!" I believe that she received the story and I know that I was punished—blissfully, I do not recall that punishment, either.

These stories were before I went to elementary school. However, I had my problems there, too. I remember that my first grade teacher and I never really hit it off—she didn't understand that for an only child, school was my social outlet. I lived for school, perhaps not for academics but for everything that went with it.

She used to draw something on the board called "the talking bird." If your name ended up under the talking bird, you had to spend recess with your nose in the corner in the hall. I believe that I spent all of first grade with my nose in the same corner and rarely saw the playground. Nowadays, this would probably violate a civil right, but it didn't affect Ms. S. in those days. The hardest thing was that the "big kids," the 5th and 6th graders, would come back to their rooms and parade past you. I recall pretending that I was a small, invisible wood animal to minimize my embarrassment.

My worst moment with Ms. S. was November 22, 1963. My parents had been strong Republicans and were not enamored of the President Kennedy or his policies. I was in first grade. A tearful Ms. S, who happened to hail from Texas called us all to her on the playground—I must have escaped her clutches that day—and broke down saying, "The President has been killed." I do not know what possessed me, but I immediately responded, "Good, now we can get a Republican." She slapped me hard across the face. Times are different.

> *"It's when you're safe at home that you wish you were having an adventure. When you're having an adventure you wish you were safe at home."*
>
> *Wilder, Thornton*

13 April 2009

> From a Southwest Airlines employee: "Welcome aboard Southwest Flight 245 to Tampa. To operate your seat belt, insert the metal tab into the buckle, and pull tight. It works just like every other seat belt; and, if you don't know how to operate one, you probably shouldn't be out in public unsupervised."

Dear Dinah,

Before I get into today's letter, I want to ask a favor of you. I will be going home for Easter and so have written a couple of days letters in advance. I plan to mail them sequentially, but if you get more than one on a day, only open according to the instructions on the envelopes. That way you will continue to have a surprise (I hope) each day.

When I got to Mississippi I tried to use the printer at the motel/hotel where they put me—however, it was useless. So, I went exploring. That—in and of itself—was interesting. I found a small printer at Office Depot for $70.00, but then I went to Wal-Mart and found one for $30. The amazing thing about this thing is that you can pack it in your suitcase. It isn't one of those $300 really tiny printers, but heck, for that price it takes up the space of two pair of gym shoes.

However, to reduce costs, the cable—which I must have a bunch of at home but none with me—cost $11.00. I am amazed that the cost of a printer is so low—I know that HP must make all their money on ink. And, I am also amazed that cables are so expensive. But, for my next assignment, I don't even plan to take a suitcase so I have to print out several letters in advance so the mail might be a bit crazy. Yet, that would be better—for me, anyway—than dealing with the airline baggage system.

I have found the air travel itself pretty enjoyable. That could be because I know that I won't be doing it forever. And, I am not saying that I like being squeezed in like a sardine. What I have enjoyed is talking to people on the planes. I must be getting to be an old person. I used to think that only old people or "losers" would get on a plane and talk. And, I'm not going to force conversation on someone who wants to read. But, I have had a kick talking to various people.

Going out to San Diego, I ended up talking for a long time to a young guy from L.A. who worked for a compressed siding company. He explained to me about how it was a mixture of wood product and cement and told me about other properties. Then we got into how his company was having to lay off people and close plants. It is just terrible—for everyone, but even for the company—when you have to lay off people who have been with you for 19 years or so. Previously he said that you could send a guy out and they could trouble shoot a problem in just a few minutes. Now, with the loss of so much corporate memory the time on-site had jumped exponentially.

Coming back from San Diego, I ended up speaking with an architect from Charlotte, N.C. We covered a lot of ground but his real passion was art. I told him that I had never been up to The Cloisters in New York and he gave me a lesson on it. Then, we discussed the Metropolitan Museum and some of its founders. He even sent me a copy of a book from his library, "Merchants and Masterpieces: The Story of the Metropolitan Museum of Art." Amazing. I was anxious to return it to him in good condition!

On another leg of the trip coming back from San Diego, I was sitting reading my medical text on TEE (transesophageal echocardiography). Two young brunette girls, very "Generation-Twitter" came down the aisle of the plane and said, "This poor guy—he gets to deal with us." They plopped down and started reading their mags. But, the older one looked over at me and said, "I bet you've never heard this!' So, she handed me her iPod and I plugged it into my Bose headsets. I said, "Oh, that's just the Veronicas." You should have seen the look on her face. But, feeling as if one good turn deserves another, I said, "Try this." I handed her my iPod and she listened for a while. "This is really good! What is it?" I said, "That is CSS (Cansei de Ser Sexy) or *Tired of Being Sexy* from Brazil. That is their song Jagger Yoga." So, I just let her listen to some more of the CSS that I had on my iPod.

To get my Mississippi license I had to fly out to Jackson, Mississippi to be fingerprinted and take a jurisprudence exam. On that flight I was studying some TEE and sat down between two guys. It turns out one was an accountant and the other was a mechanic. I had no more than gotten settled into my seat when the mechanic said, "that is one really long word. What is it?" So, instead of reading, for the next hour—which started with a brief explanation of how we use these sound waves to image the heart—I talked with these guys about medicine, my practice and then their lives. It was a very engaging discussion.

On my way back from Jackson, I ended up sitting next to a woman who does environmental testing—primarily in water. She was fascinating, living out on a small farm in Washington State. We talked about the different climates and since she was a gardener we had a lot to talk about. I don't know how we got to it, but we ended up talking about opera nightmares. When we went to Paris, we took Cecily to a rarely staged opera by Berlioz entitled Les Troyen (The Trojans). Since Cecily is such a purist for historical accuracy, she was absolutely scandalized by the fact that the sets were minimalistic and the Greeks wore one red ski glove and the Trojans wore one white one—or, possibly, I have it backward. All I remember is Cecily going on and on about this and that all night and I am thinking, "I paid that much for these tickets for this?" This lady had a similar, equally tragic opera experience, I recall.

I guess I could distill some of this into a recent encounter I had at the gym in here in Greenville, M.S. Some guy started talking to me and after a while he asked me what I do. I told him and he said, "You don't seem like a doctor. I mean, I can talk to you." I say this mainly because I think it reflect really badly on my profession. Doctors should be approachable and easy to speak with. Getting information out of patients is so important that we have to have some degree of social skill.

I also finished a medical management course down in Tampa. One of the things they emphasized was that if you are interviewing for a job was that you should be nice to the secretary. Imagine! If you are a 30 or 40 or 50 year old man or woman and have to be told to be nice to people, well, I just don't know that there is much remediation that can be done for you. You shouldn't just be doing it to get a job.

> *Heard on Southwest Airlines just after a very hard landing in Salt Lake City: The flight attendant came on the intercom and said, "That was quite a bump, and I know what y'all are thinking. I'm here to tell you it wasn't the airline's fault, it wasn't the pilot's fault, it wasn't the flight attendant's fault, it was the asphalt."*

14 April 2009

> *You might be a redneck if, when your mother goes to the bathroom she says "Ya'll come look at this before I flush it!"*
>
> *Jeff Foxworthy*

Dear Dinah,

We have reached that stage in my Mom's dementia/Alzheimer's, whatever you wish to call it, that a certain degree of embarrassment goes with the territory. The problem is that Mom still looks really good and doesn't act deranged. So, something will just come out of her mouth that makes you go, "I think I am just going to die." Couple this with her naturally inquisitive nature and it does lead to great experiments in social interaction.

I could begin with the relatively trivial example at our local Mexican restaurant. Since Mom lived in the southwest for so long, she doesn't have much experience with black people. Mexicans, yes. Blacks, no. So, all of us are out eating one night at Broncos and a young couple comes in with their baby. They were all white and the baby was black. My god, you would never have thought that such a calcified neck was so flexible. Mom just stared and stared. I knew it was coming.

It is just like when you have seen someone at church for 10 years but don't know their name. Cecily had an uncanny knack for asking, really loud just after you had made your salutation, "Oh, Hi, it is sooo good to see you." "What's her name? I want to know her name." "Run along and don't interrupt while I am talking!"

Well, this is the sandwich generation equivalent of that problem. Really loud Mom said, "Whose baby is that?" I mean, if the question didn't get you her hardness of hearing would put the final stake in your heart. So, you try to temporize. "I don't know Mom. I don't know those people." This is absolutely not sufficient. "Whose baby do you think it is?" Louder. "I don't know." Maybe I can spin this. Avoid complications like interracial marriage, living together, adoption. "I think they are just baby-sitting." "Well, I don't." God, I am glad that I was done. Very quickly I said, "Paula, I am going to the bathroom. Will you stay with Mom a minute?" Gone in 60 seconds! For 60 minutes.

This goes quite well with the fact that Mom's caregiver—who just happens to be black—is Mom's primary caregiver. Fortunately, Mom is not racist—just nosy. She loves Lucy and possibly more importantly, Lucy and her daughter love Mom. One day, though, I came home and Mom said to me, almost whispering, "Steven, there are a lot of black people in South Carolina." "Yes," I said, "there are. A lot more than in New Mexico." But, then I looked at the television. It was set on BET. I mean, no wonder Mom thought there were a lot of black people here—she only had blacks in her living room!

The redeeming aspect of Mom's interest in racial issues—I mean, you have to remember that she grew up dirt poor in West Texas, talk about forsaken country—is that she is obtuse to the questions she poses to everyone. We went out to Rice for Cecily's graduation and were greeting some of Cecily's classmates following the ceremony. One guy in particular, whom we had grown attached to over 4 years and who specifically had helped Cecily move in as a freshman was speaking with us. Then, horror of horrors, I could see that glint in Mom's eyes. I just knew she was going to say something. I just was unsure as to how bad it would be.

"What's your name?" Well, we can survive that. He answered with a generically Mexican surname. Lopez. Gonzalez. Sanchez. Whatever. Brightening, Mom immediately got into her story. "I am from New Mexico. We have a lot of Spanish people there." Yada, yada. She also always qualifies things as being Spanish, never Mexican. I have tried until I am blue in the face saying that being Mexican is not bad. It means, that . . . you are from Mexico! They are not Spaniards, who happen to be from Spain. But, I guess that the worst thing you could call someone out in Pecos, Texas in the 30's was a Mexican, so old, "gracious" habits die hard. Fortunately, this boy was extremely gracious and we retrieved Mom.

My personal favorite was when the girls planned my 50th birthday party. My birthday is in June and the party was in August. The way this worked out was that they were overseas until then and they and Paula wanted everyone to be there. So, they had my surprise party in August. People asked me if I was surprised and I had to say, "Yes." I mean, when your birthday is in June and you get your surprise birthday party in August—would you be surprised?

Well, anyway, I am sure that I will spoil a bit of the surprise when I tell you that Carter had a good friend, Raj, who is Indian (Indian subcontinent). Raj is an absolutely fabulous chef among other skills and he helped Carter put together all of the food for the party. The two of them worked like dogs on the preparations, Raj certainly going above and beyond the call of duty as a friend.

Well, the party starts and everything is going swimmingly, people eating and drinking, it was a beautiful sunny Sunday afternoon. So, we have an interlude and Carter is standing with Paula and Raj and I take Mom over to introduce her to him. She looks at him and doesn't recognize his name. I don't know how it came up but he said, "I am Indian." Well, she just beamed. Rarely have I seen her smile like that. She said, "Have you met Gandhi?"

However, some of this even reaches family members. Dementia—at least in Mom's case—has significantly affected her ability to function with time. As you know, Paula used to work at corporate headquarters for Sears in Chicago. What used to be Sears Tower, soon to be Willis Tower. Mom asked her the other day if she worked there in the 30's.

She also told Lucy the other day that Carter didn't know who she (Mom) is—that Carter hadn't seen her since she was a baby (as you know, not the case!). Carter is an incredibly dutifully granddaughter. One day, she even was discussing dates with me and in her calculation she was 60 and I was 65. I have heard of the new math, listened to Tom Lehrer, but this is truly crazy!

One day at the hospital I was talking with a nurse and we were discussing Alzheimer's in our parents. Her father died of it and her mother had it. I told her that I was in the same situation—that Dad had died of it and that Mom had it, too. She said, "aren't you absolutely terrified that you will get it?" I said, "truthfully, I don't give it a thought. I don't worry about it." She said, "That is just so remarkable. I don't know how you do that!" Only because I was feeling honest that day and didn't want to commit a sin of omission that I said, "I'm adopted."

Fortunately, we are at a good stage now. Mom went through a very unhappy period. She was angry and depressed. Now, she is surrounded by those who love her and her mood is good almost all the time. We no longer fight over her car—like we did when she was driving—and she doesn't worry about the bills anymore. I am so thankful that she has reached this stage where she seems content. Moreover, I am most thankful that we have Lucy—without her, right now, our lives would be impossible. Personally, as long as I can, we will just venture down this road if it keeps Mom out of a nursing home.

> *"I laugh, I love, I hope, I try, I hurt, I need, I fear, I cry. And I know you do the same things too, So we're really not that different, me and you."*
>
> *Colin Raye*

15 April 2009

"Perhaps host and guest is really the happiest relation for father and son."

Evelyn Waugh

Dear Dinah,

I thought I would tell you a little about Dad and his family. He was born in Broken Bow, Nebraska and from what he told me about it, "Steven, there is no excuse for Nebraska—it is hot as hell in the summer and cold as a witch's tit in the winter." First chance he had, he left Nebraska with no intention of ever going back. His family was of rural stock which is a very nice euphemism for saying they were dirt poor.

To this day I do not know what his Dad did—I guess he did whatever he could, I believe. In marked contrast, his mother was the bedrock of the family, a very good Christian woman when that terminology exemplified all that was best of American values. There was dad's older brother, a pair of twins—brother and sister—an older sister and then dad, the baby. When Dad was 13 his mother died from complication of diabetes and he was the only one still living at home. This sent his father into a cycle of bankruptcy, alcoholism and depression.

Dad always liked to draw and had applied to work with Walt Disney in California. He received a letter encouraging him to come out to Los Angeles so he and another guy hopped the rail and with their few funds headed to L.A. by train as hoboes. One night en route, they got "rolled," money taken and dumped off in Albuquerque.

Dad ended up getting a job for the The Albuquerque Journal. At first, he organized all the Mexican kids in several neighborhoods to distribute papers. Then, he worked his way up to working in the office where he wanted to get into advertizing.

He had a winning way but grew up rough. I know that at one point he did get the money to buy a car. Unfortunately, he had a way of going out drinking and forgetting where he parked it. He got into the habit of reporting it to the police as stolen. However, after about the third or fourth time that he did this, he got called into the police department and received a stern warning that they were not a car retrieval service.

World War II came along and Dad entered in the enlisted part of the Army. However, he always had dreams of flying and ultimately became a mustang—I believe that is the term for it—proceeding from enlisted ranks into the officer corps. Not atypically, on his assignment sheet he was asked for preferences for service and he put, "anywhere but Texas." Guess where he was assigned.

It was in Pecos, Texas that he met mom. I have heard the story from her perspective. Apparently, she and her mother were in the soda shop and she said that "the most gorgeous man I had ever seen walked in." Certainly, it was attraction if not love at first sight on mom's part. Likewise, I believe that Mom caught dad's eye because they started dating shortly thereafter. I do not know how they got "set up," but I can't imaging it is hard to track down a woman in Pecos, Texas. Even now.

There was one bump in the road. Dad got sent out of town for several weeks and his buddy, Claus, asked to borrow his car. Dad was particularly proud of this one—I don't know what it was, but it was a dozy. Unbeknownst to dad, Claus asked Mom out and they went out a few times. Tooling around the burb of Pecos in Dad's car, living it up. So, Dad comes back to town, eager to see his girl and pulls up in his car, jumps out and Mom exclaims, "How nice—Claus let you borrow his car!" It must have been a very hot Texas night!

Dad did a god-awful number of missions in the Pacific as a bomber pilot as the war wore on. Guam was one of the places he was based and took sorties out of. They had them live in Quonset huts which were double-layered, an inside shell and an outside shell. Apparently, some big rats used to live between these shells and would come and forage in the barracks at night. Dad said that you could hear their nails scraping on the wooden floors all night and it would drive everyone crazy.

So, one night everyone in the barracks resolved to get in bed, sit up with their pistols and turn off the lights. When the noise from the rats was maximal, they would open fire on the floor and eliminate the problem. They followed their plan to perfection but without the intended result. After they stopped shooting, they turned on the light. The floor was riddled with bullets and destroyed but not a single rat was killed. Not even any blood. Don't try this at home.

After the war, Dad went to work for American Furniture—I think he might have started there before the war and in those days they would hold your position. Companies were so different then. He was there until he got recalled for Korea. In Korea, instead of flying the big planes—bombers—he flew small planes, light reconnaissance, over enemy lines with a photographer. Talk about a change. Then, after the war he got out of the military and went back to work with American. I was adopted shortly thereafter.

Even later in life, however, Dad had a super high regard for the military. It is not hard to imagine that—for this man who lost his mother early—the sense of organization and discipline he received from the military served as a surrogate parent for him. It did make home life difficult at times, thought.

For example, when he wanted to spend "quality time," he found it hard to do. He was an absolutely incredible woodworker and I loved to see him work. However, sometimes I wanted to do stuff. So, he would say, "Let's build something." I would get so excited. Then, he would give me a list of things to assemble. These 2 x 4's, nails, rasps, vices. Get the table all set. Once everything would be set, he would do everything himself. Needless to say, this did not lend itself to many repeat performances as I reached my teen years.

The same thing could be said of dad's golf passion. With his job at American being retail and having to work Monday and Friday nights and Saturdays, he had little time off. Only as I get older do I appreciate how hard that guy worked; no longer do I feel that it is trite when people say that you only appreciate your parents when you have your own children. But, because of this lack of time he couldn't get into camping or fishing or other outdoor stuff that I dreamed of.

So, dad's cathedral was that of the links. Sundays you could find him worshiping on the golf course and I would sometimes go with him. However, after dropping his membership at Four Hills, we played public courses and I would say, "Can I just play 9 holes?" He would always say, "If I pay for 18 holes, you are going to play 18 holes." I know that was when I was young, maybe 10 or 11 and it totally turned me off to golf. Maybe that was when I started agreeing with Mark Twain that golf is a good walk, ruined.

But, then again, as much as Dad loved me I know that I was probably not the child he had hoped for. He always told me that his dream was to be a golfer and orthodontist. Now, I realize that that was probably his dream for me. So, to have a bookworm of a son, a non-athlete, was probably something that took him a long time to come to terms with. I see some fathers and sons who are so close and have such similar interests that I cannot help but become jealous at times. Maybe for this reason I feel lucky that I had girls—I would not want to disappoint on both ends of the spectrum, being a bad Dad to a son as I might have been to my father. But, I do miss him terribly.

> "Whenever I get gloomy with the state of the world, I think about the arrivals gate at Heathrow Airport. General opinion's starting to make out that we live in a world of hatred and greed, but I don't see that. It seems to me that love is everywhere. Often it's not particularly dignified or newsworthy, but it's always there—fathers and sons, mothers and daughters, husbands and wives, boyfriends, girlfriends, old friends. When the planes hit the Twin Towers, as far as I know none of the phone calls from the people on board were messages of hate or revenge—they were all messages of love. If you look for it, I've got a sneaky feeling you'll find that love actually is all around."
>
> *Love Actually*

16 April 2009

> *"I want to die in my sleep like my grandfather . . . Not screaming and yelling like the passengers in his car."*
>
> Will Shriner

Dear Dinah,

    To a certain degree you can define a man by the cars he drives. I say this with a degree of trepidation, since I am driving a Honda Pilot. Nonetheless, I thought I might review for you some of my vehicular history.
    My first car was my yellow, six-speed 1967 Mustang. Dad got that for me when I was a junior in high school. Goodbye waiting at the bus stop, freezing, stomping my feet. I had wheels. The acquisition was made in a circuitous manner. There was a fairly prominent pimp in town called Prince Billy Jack. I mean, I don't know that that was his advertised profession but that was his rep.
    The Prince was in the American and was talking to Dad. Apparently, he had some reasons for going on the road for a while—I believe it was IRS issues from what I can deduce at this late stage—and he was cutting overhead—girls, apartments, cars. My car was one that one of his favorite girls drove and he was getting rid of it. Quickly, a deal was struck for cash. Dad would pay him this much and the car was his.
    The disadvantage of driving this car was that it looked fast but had the engine of a Yugo in it. Maybe that was Dad's plan. Worse yet, I thought and knew that I was dapper so I affected an English driving cap. I don't know if you remember that but I do. I mean, the 70's had styles that were horrid enough but you put this with my haircut then and the cap and it just doesn't bear thinking about. I suspect you could make it worse by putting something like "Muskrat Love" by Captain and Tennille on the 8-track, but not much.
    The best thing about my Mustang was that it spirited me for my dates with Tina. That was quite important since mother never really took to any girl that I went out with. For the year that I dated Tina in high school, I would say, "I'm going out tonight with Tina." The response would invariable be, "Oh, that little German girl." This went on all year. It wasn't until I went to college and started dating other girls that Mom finally said,

"Oh, I saw Tina today in a store—she looks really good." Thanks Mom, thanks.

I took my mustang to college where—as Dad predicted—my hubcaps would be stolen. So, I ended up driving without for several years and then—when I went to medical school, the car was suddenly confiscated from me. It would be too much that I take my mustang to the south side of Chicago. So, Dad took the mustang and I got a Ford Maverick. I believe that I have told you in another letter about how I used to drive through Chicago without heat listening to my French rock and roll, looking through the side window. Yes, that Mustang.

When Paula and I moved to Philly, I rode my bike to the hospital so to cut costs, I needed to sell the car. I needed the money and didn't want to pay the insurance. Anyway, the brakes were going on the Maverick and I didn't want to fix them. I put an ad in the paper and some poor guy—I believe a recent immigrant from China—answered and wanted the car. He said, "Car OK?" I said, "Car, OK." I don't know what he wanted for $1000, but he took the car. However, a few days later he called and either asked or said—I am not sure, "Brakes work." I said, "Brakes work." That was the last that I heard of him. Paula still holds me ethically responsible for the accident she presumes that he had—to which I plead guilty—but, having no money made my ethics much more elastic in those days.

In the anesthesia department at Penn, we had a scheduler who honored requests in inverse proportion to how many requests you put in. Some people had multiple requests and had few if any honored. I had one request for Dr. Prevosnick. "Steve, I don't have a car—don't give me an away rotation until my last month." I got it. And, that was when I got my woody station wagon. I never knew that a person could be so happy about embracing suburban existence. Ah, my gateway to having my gonads removed medically. My wonderful, fake wood-sided Caprice station wagon.

The story that comes to mind with this car was the time Mom and Dad came to visit us in Washington when I was in the Air Force. Paula and I were in the front seat, Carter and Cecily flanked Mom in the back. Someone cut me off on the beltway and I restrained myself admirably—and atypically—in these circumstances. Carter piped in with her little high shrill voice, "That's a f***ing bastard!" In the rearview mirror I could see the blood drain from Mom's face as she looked at Carter and said, "What's that, sweetheart?" "Oh, Daddy says that anybody who drives like that is a f***ing bastard, Grand Mommy ." Then she gave a big smile.

Carter that is. My ears got boxed by Mom and I received a long lecture from Paula.

When I got out of the Air Force, I felt that I had to do what every red-blooded male did and got a big fun car. I got a BMW 740 iL. I loved that car. In retrospect, I would never do that again. I didn't know—being from New Mexico—that in South Carolina you pay a personal property tax on your car. I almost had a heart attack when I got my first bill.

Worse yet, one time we took a trip to Charleston in my car with the sweet smelling leather seats. From the back seat, Cecily said, "I haf go potty." Damn. We just stopped. First Paula, then me. Then Carter. "Hold on sweetheart. Just a bit." This went on for about 20 miles, "Haf go potty," with my trying to get a bit further. I was tired of the 3 ½ hour trip from Charleston taking 5 hours. Abruptly, though, an unusual scent wafted through the car and Carter interjected, "Don't worry Daddy, I don't think you need to stop now. Cecily already went poo poo." Needless to say, we had to leave her entire outfit at the side of the road. Then, the major decision was smell or temperature. Every time I rolled the windows up, the smell was horrible. Or, if we rolled them down, we froze (it was winter).

I have had other cars through the years. Even with a few luxury models thrown in, my most expensive car was the Volvo that I bought for Carter. Like all parents who are concerned about their first child driving, I really wanted her to be in a safe car. However, I didn't want to spend an arm and a leg for a car. After much deliberation, I bought her a used Volvo station wagon. She hated it which only endeared it more to me. She said, "OK, you drive it to me—I will be in Spartanburg today." So, I took this car that I still remember that I paid $3,000 for and drove the back road to Spartanburg. There is a big hill with a steep incline on Hwy 29 which the car just couldn't make. I hit the gas and it tried and it tried and then the engine burst into flames. It was totally torched. Actually, it was very impressive—not as a car but as a form of pyrotechnics. The car was taken to salvage. That proved to be a 10 mile ride for $3000.

Ultimately, I ended up with a paid—off Range Rover which I did love. It was a great car. But, at one point it starting listing to the right. I mean, at something like 30 to 40 degrees. I took it to the dealership and they said, "Oh, yes. This is the pneumatic stabilization system." When I asked them how much it would be to repair, they said it would be between $2,500 and $10,000. So, I drove around on the tilt for several days, contemplating my options. Then, I decided that I would do what the rest of America is doing. Buy a well-built American car—a Japanese car. That is when I got my Honda Pilot. I have never regretted my decision.

> *"Men are superior to women, for one thing they can urinate from a speeding car"*
>
> *Will Durst*

17 April 2009

Written at Memphis International Airport

"Storytelling and copulation are the two chief forms of amusement in the South. They're inexpensive and easy to procure."

Robert Penn Warren

Dear Dinah,

Since I am leaving Greenville, Mississippi, I want to try to summarize my impressions of the place for you. To begin with, when I travel overseas I usually do extensive research on the place I plan to visit—museums, operating hours, sites and such. Needless to say, for Greenville the list of "things" to do that you can find on the web is not what I would describe as extensive. Yet, I found Greenville to be a true treasure of people and places.

That said, Greenville has what so many small towns have in the South—a street that you drive down and go, "Oh my God. Could I live here?" We have one in Gaffney and one of the anesthesiologists I worked with in Greenville said that his wife said the same thing the first time they drove into Greenville. In fact, our experiences were rather parallel. It used to drive both of us crazy that people wouldn't give us addresses for businesses and that numbers weren't often posted. People would just say, "It is across from old Broncos, you know in that shopping center where Dominos was before they moved? Right." Well, not really, but I will make it work.

Strangely, I believe that this is a defining test for those who will actually be able to survive the Darwinian selection process involved in surviving in a small town. You have to get around without most of the things that have been invented since the modern city was developed in the Middle Ages. In addition, it poses quite interesting cognitive issues concerning how people process mapping in their brains. Yet, I wander. Never have done that before.

Arriving in Greenville on a Sunday night, I had my list of things to do—eat at Doe's Eat Place, get a gym membership and hear some blues. My first day of work was predictable—I had the patient who had the recent heart attach, the stinky belly case and on Wednesday night when I took call I was made to feel at home with a gun shot wound to the belly. I am amazing how these perpetrators get around. From Chicago to Philly to D.C. to Baltimore, further south, these cases invariably have the same story. "I was reading my Bible at that phone booth—in those pre-cell phone days—at 4 AM when them two dudes come up and just shoot me for no reason!" I am firmly convinced that if we were to catch "them two dudes" we would eliminate most violent crime in America.

Monday I made one of my major discoveries—Tabb's BBQ Restaurant. I had been told that one of the nurses in the OR and her husband had a BBQ restaurant and that I should try it. Well, over the course of my two weeks here it has become my second home. It has a big sunny window where I have done my writing—much more exciting than being in my hotel room—and they have plied me with endless amounts of tea. When I have eaten there, Peggy and Rusty have treated me like family and I have sat at their big table in the middle of the room with them and all their friends visiting. Add to that that their BBQ is great and I was in heaven.

I went to the YMCA and they graciously gave me a "comp" membership since I am a member in South Carolina. I just remarked that they had a really nice addition and the lady there said, "You have to tell that to our director." So, he and I chatted for a long time. I told him that my question—not to sound too ignorant—was why everything up here was called "Delta this" and "Delta that." I always thought that a delta was much closer to the mouth of the river. All I could do was to speculate was that this was true in geologic time.

He referred me to "McCormick's Bookstore," where others had told me that I should meet Hugh McCormick, the resident repository—himself, not his bookstore—for all knowledge Greenvillian in nature. Driving over there, I met said Mr. McCormick. Figuring that I would immediately ingratiate myself to him I asked if I could use his computer because I wanted to look up a book on Amazon. Fortunately, I was not thrown out on my keester for this.

He has a magnificent bookstore in two parts. The first part is full of wonderful books, emphasizing Mississippi history, photography and literature. Greenville was quite a nexus for literature at a certain point in time, featuring writers including Shelby Foote, Hodding Carter and Walker Percy. The second part of the store is full of artifacts, photographs and other things significant in Greenville's history. The big story here—to this day—is the 1927 flood which caused major devastation and political changes which were permanent. A recent book discusses this—and is popular—but Hugh pulls out a weathered copy with hundreds of yellow tags hanging out of the pages indicating where he has found inaccuracies. He is not a fan.

One night I drove over to the afore mentioned Doe's Eat Place. Doe's has quite a history in Greenville, having served as a grocery store at the turn of the century, I believe bootlegging was involved at some stages and then gradually the clientele switched from predominantly black to white—probably as the prices went up. But, it is in what you could euphemistically call a transitional neighborhood. If Doe's moved, though, I believe it would lose all of its charm.

You enter the restaurant through the kitchen and get ready for truly one of the great steak experiences to be had. I ordered a filet because I was warned that the other cuts were huge and I still couldn't eat it all. They also—and I have no idea why or how—serve tamales. I just don't associate tamales with the Mississippi Delta, being from New Mexico, but they were out of this world.

The previous day at the hospital, one of the nurses told me that she would not eat at Doe's without her husband—for fear I suspect. I told her that I would be comfortable eating at Doe's without her husband. But, the next day they asked me how I got there and I told them I just put it in my GPS and went—and waited for "the youths to part in the street," they said, "What streets did you go down?" When I said, "Alexander and then Nelson," they were fit to be tied. "You just can't trust them GPS's."

When I was in college I was astounded how the Jewish kids I knew would play what I called, "Jewish geography." They would get together and say, "Did you know so and so?" and it was rare that through summer camps, Hillel or some other tangential organization they couldn't figure out someone they knew in common. Well, something somewhat similar happened to me in Greenville, but with a much more Southern Gothic twist.

One of my best friends is a surgeon who attended a small southern college. His roommate from freshman year was from Greenville and returned to Mississippi to finish college at Ole Miss. This surgeon asked me if I would call his long-lost roommate and say hello for him and I was more than willing to oblige. When I called his house, a woman answered with the most beautiful, broad southern accent which I had heard in quite a while. I am an aficionado for accents. Old Charleston has a very patrician accent which is dying out. Gaffney where we live is modified country. This was a very slow, broad and sweet accent. "Yes, sirrrrr," she would say. I have no idea how many "r's" to put in there.

Well, the next night this man called me back and we had a long talk. Or, to be more accurate, I had a listen. "Lardy, he is a talker!" Nonetheless, I heard long vignettes about the floods, prominent citizens, how the city had change. It was fascinating. On probably about the 10th time after trying to bid him goodbye, I was able to get off the phone. So, the next day I go to the OR and told someone who I had been speaking with. They said, "Be careful." I was perplexed. "Why?" "Well, about 5 years ago his aunt was found brutally slain on her sun porch and he was a prime suspect at the time. No one has ever been caught."

My last night I wanted to go to the Blues Bar. I knew—not being a complete moron—that the music would probably start late but I drove by about 8 PM and asked when it would start. They said, "Oh, around 10 PM tonight." It was then and there that I realized how old I am. Thursday night is no longer a party night for me. When I have to get up work with patients the next day, I just can't be out at a blues bar the night before. "Thanks, I said." I drove off, disappointed, but ready for bed. I had a wonderful time in Greenville.

> *"I think, weirdly, it almost takes an outsider to be able to—with no cynicism—look at small-town America and realize how fantastic it is."*
>
> Michael Davies

18 April 2009

> *"When my cats aren't happy, I'm not happy. Not because I care about their mood but because I know they're just sitting there thinking up ways to get even."*
>
> Percy Bysshe Shelley

Dear Dinah,

With three kids of your own I am sure that you have plenty of pet stories. You really can't escape them—no matter how hard you try—when you are rearing children. For some reason we think, or perhaps I should only speak for myself, that having pets teaches children a sense of responsibility. If this were the only reason, though, you could have those electronic pets of which the Japanese have become so enamored. I incline more to the approach of the French artist, Gérard de Nerval, who had a pet lobster he used to walk along the streets of Paris with a blue ribbon as a leash.

In spite of my druthers, though, I have always had more conventional pets. My first dog was Charlie Weaver, a big happy basset hound who was full of life. The problem was that he was so full of life that he wanted to share this desire—which, in point of fact it was—with everyone who entered our backyard on California Street. I couldn't have friends over to play because as soon as you entered the yard, Charlie Brown started humping you. Mom and Dad tried "the ultimate solution" but I believe that he had had a taste of the good life, so to speak, and this did not mitigate the problem. He was given away and we migrated to smaller dogs. They may have been full of the same desires as Charlie Weaver, but you could just knock them away. I understand how they feel. That is the way I feel as a small man entering a bar.

We had several delightful dachshunds before my parents switched to schnauzers. Talk about a psychotic breed. I know that they didn't know me when I would come home from college or medical school, but whenever I would return these dogs barked relentlessly.

During training, Paula and I didn't have pets, living in shall I say confined circumstances. However, when we moved to D.C. and the girls had come along, we acquired our first set—a pair of cockatiels which we named for some friends of ours in Philly, Mark and Eva.

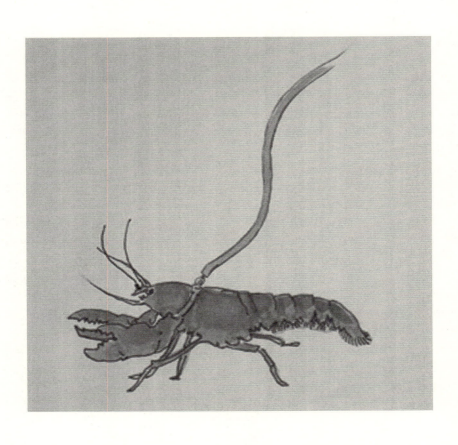

Mark was a brute and over the years that we had these birds, Mark pecked the back of Eva's head so much that she ended up becoming completely baldheaded. Not speaking bird, I don't know if she deserved it, but I did seem excessive. And, it didn't correspond to their human namesakes, because in human life, Mark would sleep in another room because light would disturb his precious Eva. Obviously, our birds did not follow the pattern.

They were survivors, though. One time they got wet—ask me how, I don't know—and Cecily decided the best cure for this was to Windex them. I would say that there a *cat*erwauling, but I don't think I should use that word for birds—let's say that they screeched like bloody hell. Yet, they did survive.

We did try our hand at rabbits, too. I had a hutch built behind our carriage house and we had one rabbit. Unfortunately, for some reason it died quite prematurely and Carter was devastated. "I never had the chance to have my photo taken with my bunny." This was a delicate issue. So, Carter and I went out and I picked up the bunny—which by this time was as rigid as plank—and said, "Come here sweetheart, let's get that picture." We have it in our album, Carter holding her beloved rabbit, both with glazed eyes.

Over time we went through turtles, fish, guinea pigs and ended up with cats. We stayed away from dogs because the yard just couldn't take that. I am allergic to cats so they have to stay outdoors. Yet, I love them. So, I play with them and then wash my hands. We started with one cat discovered one night in the middle of the winter—Paula and Carter heard a tremendous wail emanating from one of our bushes and lo and behold, it was a microscopic cat. Saved, it became our most significant cat, "Beautiful," for her exquisite white coat. We then got two more cats—adopted, I suspect—named in complete politically correct southern terminology, "Blackie" and "White-face." Duh. In this case, however, any retribution for slavery was vindicated because Blackie chased off Whiteface and became king of the yard.

Blackie was an amazing cat. He loved to cat-around and fight and be with the ladies. One morning, he came back with part of a tail and his left ear bent forward. He was summarily emasculated but like Charlie Weaver, one you have tasted of the fountain, you always like the clear water. So, while his fights became less frequent, they were not eliminated.

Blackie was our cat but ultimately chose to live with others. Our neighbors, Jim and Linda, but I must say particularly Jim, fed Blackie steak and tuna and all sorts of other tidbits that he was never likely to get at our house—by this point Paula was cooking vegetarian dishes. Cats are highly intelligent and Blackie made a rational decision; were it only the case that humans such as yours truly could move from house to house to eat, too. Then, he ended up like a lounge lizard strolling over mid-day to Shirley's house for warm cream. He would come by to visit, but then would soon enough be off again.

For a while, Cecily used to take a guinea pig, a cockatiel and Beautiful up into Mrs. Etang's tree—it was like the lion lying down with the lamb. For some reason all four of them were able to play together happily in the ginkgo tree—or, at least no one ever got eaten.

One winter, we did take in a stray cat that was given away at the door to Wal-Mart. That should have been foreshadowing enough. It was cold and the girls begged and begged and I said that they could put it in the upstairs "garbage" room—everyone has a room where everything you don't need get stuffed. Well the cat ended up in there. It would not have been much of a problem save for the fact that about 2 weeks later Paula and Carter would wake up each morning with terrible little bites about their legs. Cecily and I were spared so we didn't really care. However, it was driving them crazy so Paula went to see a local doctor who told her that she had fleas. Well, the cat was out, the house was fumigated and I was under strict orders—on fear of never having sex again—not to talk about my wife being a fleabag.

Our last major incursion with animals was when—for some reason—I saw a couple of our white cats playing in the garden and I decided that it would be good to "decorate the yard" with white cats. So, I think over a few months we acquired 10 white cats. It was beautiful, seeing all these beautiful babes playing in our green bushes and strolling on our gray gravel. This is as close to being a Hugh Heffner that I will ever be.

Yet, tragedy struck in the heart of Eden. Some were hit by cars, some disappeared. Our numbers diminished. Finally, we were left with Beautiful and she was looking poorly. After watching her for a couple of days, Paula found her moping around the back door and petted her—but, she was really not responsive. Paula drove her to the vet—something unheard of in her prime, when she would have fought you to not get in the car—and she rode in Paula's arms. Getting there, however, Paula carried her into the vet's office and Beauty looked in, saw a big dog and promptly had a seizure and died in Paula's arms. It turned out that she cardiomyopathy from heart worms and would not have survived. Yet, it seemed such an ignominious end to our most wonderful cat.

"In nine lifetimes, you'll never know as much about your cat as your cat knows about you."

Michel de Montaigne

19 April 2009

> *"You are drunk Sir Winston, you are disgustingly drunk. 'Yes, Mrs. Braddock, I am drunk. But you, Mrs. Braddock are ugly, and disgustingly fat. But, tomorrow morning, I, Winston Churchill will be sober."*
>
> *Winston Churchill*

Dear Dinah,

Today has been a very busy day in the operating room and I am pretty tired. However, I shall not give up on my quest to provide you with a Decameron of your very own stories. Therefore, I will transport you—and me—to a more pleasant time when Paula and I went together to France on our very first vacation together.

We started in Brussels. As all transatlantic flights are, this one had been exhausting but perhaps more so for me than for Paula. If I remember correctly—and it is sad to say that it was more years ago than the girls are old—we settled in to watch the movie and my headphones didn't work. This was "back in the day" when you received those plastic tubes that you had to stick into holes in the armrests—not this newfangled iPod, everyone watch their own video and bring their own Bose noise-cancelling headsets.

Calling the stewardess aside, she said, "Oh that is just too bad!" And, I mean, it was so atypical versus today. She really meant it. She said, "Let me see what I can do," and disappeared. Returning in about 10 minutes, she said, "Well, there are no other seats in economy or first class—would you mind sitting at the piano bar for a while?" So, she took me up the helical staircase to the Promised Land and there were people sitting around listening to someone playing a piano, drinking and having a great time. Within a few minutes, I was friends with everyone there and was plied with drinks for the duration of the flight. It was only for landing that I was recast into that Inner Circles of Hell again, economy, but that didn't last too long.

In Brussels, we had a day to relax before we headed off to France. So, we ambled around, did some window shopping—as much as a medical student could do—and then sat down to have one of those enormous glass steins of beer. I don't know what it was but within 5 minutes I had some horrible reaction to the beer—the hops, my fatigue, don't know. Anyway,

I had a terrible asthma attack and had left my inhaler in our chamber. So, with me huffing and wheezing we headed as quickly as my pink puffy cheeks could get me there to our hotel. It felt that we just made it and I took several puffs on the inhaler—probably more than a few—because Paula said that it felt like my heart would pound out of my chest. It was going like 180 beats per minutes. But, I was breathing! Yea!

The next day, we drove into northern France, going through Reim and then to Paris. In Paris, since Paula was the one with the job and the one with the credit card, I was given scant attention by any single doorman, check-in clerk or anyone else. I was viewed very dimly and I must have been viewed as being only service personal myself—and you can imagine the service they suspected me to provide. I will not get into that, save that it did very little for my ego, particularly when—knowing the French—they were thinking, "Ah, why would sheee pay for dat little shit, wheeen weee aaaah aaalll heeere?" If you didn't know it, I am completely fluent in insult.

We stayed in the Holiday Inn on Place de la Republique which truly doesn't sound too inspiring, but at that particular time it had just been redone and the rooms were very luxurious, with very comfortable bathrooms and it opened on a beautiful central courtyard. Moreover, in those distant, wonderful pre-Euro days when a dollar actually had value, I believe we were getting something on the order of 8 francs to the dollar so we were living like royalty on not too much money.

From Paris, we drove—in a very ambling way—down through the central part of France, ending up in Avignon. On the way, and I must remind you that this was the early 80's, "le Fast Food had not made major in-roads into France and the French observed their mealtimes. For some reason we would stay up every night late, sleep in, get in the car around 10 AM and want to eat at 2 PM. This just did not go with their schedules. Every day my blood sugar would dip at this time and I would have to eat. Did either of us think to change our schedules? No. One day, in a total tizzy we entered a restaurant at 2 PM in a small town. The propriétaire looked at me, pointed to the clock and shook her head, tragically. Mustering my best French, I looked back at her—and the look in my eyes must have scared her—I too nodded in the affirmatively and said, "Doit mange" M'aide!" Either from fear or bafflement or amusement, she disappeared and returned with two sandwiches made from baguettes which were as hard as stones (literally), with a piece of ham on them that you could read Braille through. But, it was food. Like a man rescued on a desert island, I sat with Paula and savored my cuisine.

We did arrive—finally—at our dream destination, St. Tropez. It was as wonderful as advertised, and being there at the end of April it wasn't totally overrun with (other) tourists! At night we could go down to the wharf and watch enormous yachts back in. One time, we saw a crew of 20 guys in identical uniforms maneuver a very large vessel in, set a table and serve a multi-course meal for a gentleman who sat on his yacht and looked at us—30 feet away, drinking our pastis, looking back at him.

One morning, I decided an adventure was in the wind. I had heard about the nude beaches in France and wanted to enjoy. Tally-ho (is that too English for this?). Anyway, we made our way to the beach and found a place where they rented windbreaks on the nude beach. Soon enough, I was participating fully in French life, so to speak. Paula demurred. However, this did not seem to be enough for me and soon I saw that what was really indicated was a champagne party on the beach. I mean, it was getting late, somewhere north of 10 AM. Soon, we had an international collection of people chattering away in 10 languages—of course, no one understood anyone else, but with the champagne flowing freely, no one really cared. We were on the beach in St. Tropez and life was good. What could be better?

Well, actually, one thing could be better and that we were shortly to discover. This was Giles. Giles was our beach guide/bum/man-about-town. He did the towels and got the champagne and such. So, of course, I wanted him to tell us where we should eat that night and go for fun. In so many words he led me to understand, "I know just what you need." Moreover, we had met an American couple living in Switzerland who were just down in St. Tropez—having saved every dime—for a few days, Peg and Tom.

We all met for drinks at Giles' appointed pre-restaurant bar and had the obligatory pastis-es. Then, after multiple hours of this, when we thought we were going to lose Tom from hunger and he started looking like he would just faint away, we finally prevailed upon Giles—it is almost 10 PM, let's eat! Off we went to the restaurant. Giles insisted on ordering for everyone in rapid-fire French. Tom was delighted when tout de suite his Soup de Poisson was served and no one else had anything. Giles obviously had taken him under his wing. Except for the fact that when the next course and the next course and the next course arrived, there was nothing for Tom. Zat eees what I ordered for you. I thought you would like it! Rarely have I seen dejection like this. Tom's picture is in the encyclopedia next to that word—dejection.

Ultimately, Giles took us to a private club and we started having a great time dancing, drinking and just carrying on. Everyone was having a blast in fact. And then, the coup de grâce. I came back from the bathroom and Paula and Peg were sitting there with Tom who looked as if his mother had died. He just received the bill for the bottle of vodka (which we were splitting). But, in 1982 his share was $100 USD. He just kept shaking his head, saying, "This can't be, this just can't be." Unfortunately, there are more things in heaven and Earth, Horatio, than are dreamt of in your philosophy.

Ultimately, we returned to Brussels to catch our flight home. Eating in one of those little seafood restaurants near the Grote Markt, the couple sitting next to us was British. We ended up talking with them all during dinner and as it turned out they invited us to join them at a private club downtown. We had an early flight but decided to do so anyway—and the only thing I remember of that night is dancing all night and a crazed Austrian man named "Willie" who was enchanted with Paula saying, "You R zee most beeeutiful woman in zzee world!" I think we made our plane by maybe one second to spare. And, that was our first trip together.

> *"Being naked approaches being revolutionary; going barefoot is mere populism"*

John Updike

20 April 2009

I ain't as good as I once was
But I'm as good once as I ever was
Maybe not be good as I once was
But I'm as good once as I ever was

Toby Keith

Dear Dinah,

    I know that I have sent you a lot of letters that are quite silly and frivolous. It seems that looking back over my life it was the things that I did that were a bit crazed and done in error are the ones which I remember. I mean, I don't remember all those nights studying and being a nerd. However, it would be disingenuous of me to try to portray myself as different that I am—and to you I couldn't do it! You have known me all my life and you know that I was pretty much a geek most of my life.

    I do remember once in high school, though, Weagley and I toilet papered your house. To my recollection, I do not think that really made you parents, especially your mom, happy. And, God, to think back on it now Jeff had the braniac idea of putting some industrial-strength toilet cleaning solvent on your front porch so that for weeks thereafter anyone coming up to visit you guys would get the scent that they were entering an airport lavatory. Only now, with the forbearance of having had children of my own, do I understand why your father didn't shoot us. It was not out of kindness. Rather, he just didn't want to waste his time in prison. Or, waste good lead.

    Over the years, though, your family has meant so much to all of us in my family. In particular, my Dad considered your father to be his best friend—and perhaps more importantly, someone he really respected. You might not know that your father really helped my father later in life, too. Dad retired from the National Guard but wouldn't get his pension until he turned 65. So, he was working for American and he filed all of his papers in his 50's and the military told him that he was something like "x" units short of being eligible for retirement. This was devastating to him, both because he had planned on this money and also because—as you know—he was pretty well decorated in both WWII and Korea for valor.

He didn't know what to do, but your father figured out a mechanism that would satisfy all of the requirements for Dad—he made him his personal assistant for certain weeks a year so he could accumulate extra points for retirement. I think my Dad even wore a sergeants uniform for these weeks—not really sure, you know how kids don't pay attention to the travails of their parents—and this must have been difficult for him, knowing how proud a man he was. But, even through this dark glass I do remember him commenting on how your father was helping him out and making things as easy for him as possible. Because of your father's assistance, Mom has that additional income at present and my father could put his mind at rest. If one family could owe another a significant moral debt, it would be ours to you.

Maybe this is what has me thinking a bit more seriously today. I have studied hard and also done some crazy things. But, as I get older—could wisdom be percolating into my noggin?—some of those old-fashioned values such as dedication, responsibility and fidelity seem even more and more important. Reviewing my life, I see how selfish and egocentric I was. Perhaps this was necessary to get through medical school and training. I do know that now residents do not work now the way we used to, with the limitations on their working hours. In those days, everything was sacrificed to your training.

In addition, perhaps it is the marital estate, but I have reached the point in my marriage with Paula where the though of losing her would be like losing a part of myself. Biblically, it always says that you will become "of one flesh." When I was younger, not only did I not believe this, I thought that at best it was allegorical and at worst pedantic. Now, the full meaning of this resonates in my life. It is like Auden say's better than I ever could about loss or potential loss:

> (S)he was my North, my South, my East and West,
> My working week and my Sunday rest,
> My noon, my midnight, my talk, my song;
> I thought that love would last for ever: I was wrong.

It is inexpressible to me how much I depend on Paula—she truly is everything to me. She is my best friend, my confidante, the person with whom I have fun. She is also the person who I can irritate and who can irritate me the most. We love, we fight, we disagree, we discuss and still—after 25 years together—I love and adore her more every day.

I think my favorite time of day, when I am not working, is when we go out on our big southern porch and have coffee together in the morning before we get our days going. One thing wonderful about living in our small town, all of the workers who come to work for us—plumbers, electricians, etc.—are not easily shocked. Therefore, when she is out there sitting in her robe and I am out in my boxers and a t-shirt, they are not scandalized. Although, I must admit that Paula exercises royal prerogative and refuses to get off of her perch—our porch swing—and I end up dealing with the workers when I am around and she isn't put together.

Yet, most of the time, she gets to deal with them on her own. To avoid the damaging rays of the sun (!), Paula does all of her gardening in long-sleeve shirts, long pants and an enormous hat that extends out about 3 feet in all directions. On more than one occasion people have come up and asked her if she knows if the woman of the house is around. With all apologies to temporary laborers, Paula makes them look like the height of sartorial taste.

In closing, for today, I send you a prayer. I have not done that up to now, but I want for you to know that I pray for you nightly and you remain close to my heart.

Traditional Buddhist Blessing and Healing Chant

*Just as the soft rains fill the streams,
pour into the rivers and join together in the oceans,
so may the power of every moment of your goodness
flow forth to awaken and heal all beings,
Those here now, those gone before, those yet to come.
By the power of every moment of your goodness
May your heart's wishes be soon fulfilled
as completely shining as the bright full moon,
as magically as by a wish-fulfilling gem.*

*By the power of every moment of your goodness
May all dangers be averted and all disease be gone.
May no obstacle come across your way.
May you enjoy fulfillment and long life.*

*For all in whose heart dwells respect,
who follow the wisdom and compassion, of the Way,
May your life prosper in the four blessings
of old age, beauty, happiness and strength.*

21 April 2009

"You know how to tell if the teacher is hung over? Movie Day."

Jay Mohr

Dear Dinah,

I thought that for today's letter, I would tell you about the time we went on an archeological dig—*en famillie*. As you probably have a pretty good idea, ideas sort of get into my mind and I feel that I have to act on them. Well, when the girls were in 6th and 7th grade I received an Earthwatch catalogue in the mail. What a treasure. Diving with the piranha in the Amazon. Entering cursed tombs in Egypt to save the scarabs. Identifying indigenous bedbug species in Tibet.

Because I have to sell my ideas to others we—as a family—finally settled on Mallorca's Copper Age led by Dr. William Waldren of Oxford. I thought this would be a no brainer in terms of getting the girl's school's approval and to a certain degree I was right—and, to a certain degree I was wrong. Cecily had Ms. Cadena, a notorious stickler who taught spelling and trucked no disagreements. Carter has kept her head down and been able to get through the year without difficulty. Cecily—probably due to my genes—was not having, shall we say, a pleasant year.

So, when Ms. Cadena heard that we wanted to pull the girls out of school for a week following the Christmas holidays she went authoritarian mode and said this would not be permitted. We finally had to appeal to the higher ups in the school administration who were able to see that an archeological dig with an Oxford professor might be a better learning experience—at least for a week—than doing spelling words in Spartanburg, S.C. Yet, I must admit—Ms. Cadena got the last laugh, because Cecily was made to pay for the rest of the year. Sigh.

Departing after my Christmas call, we flew to Madrid and immediately on to Mallorca, ending up in Deya. Deya is the Mediterranean equivalent of the artsy place I love in Mexico, San Miguel de Allende. Robert Graves, who wrote *I, Claudius*, lived there after "The Great War," and Anaïs Nin also visited and wrote there. The topography is steep hills with olive and orange groves overlooking the sea. Stunning would be an inadequate description.

We had reservations at the magnificent La Residencia—where we were a few weeks after Dodi and Di were there. Constructed from two abandoned stone farmhouses, the estate has grown and spread and we certainly felt pampered while we were there. We had flown into Deya and checked into the hotel on New Year's Eve, 1997. Everyone was totally out of it from jet lag but we wanted to enjoy our New Year's celebration in the hotel restaurant.

Mustering all of our energies, we rallied and made our way downstairs and into the restaurant. The food was good but what still stands out in my mind was the exquisite presentation and detailing. To this day I can still recall the little faces they made in the condiments on the girl's deserts, smiling clown faces, in contrast to our towering gateaux. I also remember the dramatic entrance of an Italian woman, joining friends, who entered grandly with her huge hair (she could have been southern!) and screaming greetings at them across the restaurant, stopped along the way to grab a candelabra from a table in passing to light her cigarette.

At midnight, the French doors to the restaurant were thrown open and we were delighted by thirty minutes of fireworks from the balcony. Of course, by this time it was just me and Paula because the girls had their faces in their plates, sleeping—or would have if we hadn't moved the plates. While we were at La Residencia we heard a wonderful New Year's day piano concert and swam, ate and were totally indolent—foo on you, Ms. Cadena.

However, after a few days, we had to depart paradise for our next adventure. We left La Residencia and headed for the Deya Archeological Museum and Research Center. This was not just a museum. Bill Waldren and his wife, Jackie, and sundry other people in addition to Earthwatch volunteers lived in the museum which was a converted mill. We lived with the girls in one dorm room with two bunk beds, among some Black Adder and other BBC VHS tapes. I knew then we were in safe territory. The other volunteers in our group had communal housing in two other large bunk rooms.

Meals were communal and we had the best time talking with other volunteers. It was a pretty equal spilt between Brits and Americans. One guy was retired US government. Another was a relatively young British newlywed couple. A girl named Christine was an archeologist back in England. My personal favorite was an adventuresome Jewish woman from New Jersey named Charlotte who also did Earthwatch trips once or twice each year.

I say that she was my favorite because she was indefatigable. Charlotte had been on one trip in the Amazon and a fish had jumped in her boat and it took them over a year back in New Jersey to figure out what sort of poison the fin had inserted into her thigh. All that time she was having paresthesias and other weird symptoms. Another time, she had been sleeping on a concrete floor on a trip doing some work at a remote village in India when her leader came and collected her. Apparently, in the next village some deranged man had been cannibalizing village children and the villagers had him cornered and were going to do unspeakable things to him—they didn't want Charlotte reporting on this!

Dr. Waldren—I use that term here—was inspirational. He was truly a man suited for his métier and his love for it showed. He just couldn't talk about archeology without bursting with enthusiasm. This might be because he came to it late and was not a sterile academic. He had been a championship figure skater, a published poet, a photography teacher and an accomplished painter. It was only at the age of 50 that he—Waldren—went to college for the first time and earned a doctorate from Oxford University and joined their faculty. He and Jackie spilt their time between Oxford and Deya and over something like 30 years he wrote the prehistorical record for this part of the Mediterranean.

Each day, we would get up, eat breakfast and then head to the field in a fleet of Range Rovers—ah, so British! There he taught us how he set up his sites, in grids, so that we could dig in our sector. We had to record each piece at each level as we uncovered it with very small tools. He wanted pre-historical material primarily. Because the Balearic Islands have been a crossroads, there was much Greek, Roman and other material. He would look at this and say, "Ah, Roman." And then toss it! Paula uncovered a Roman die from gaming and another in our party found what the group dubbed an early "Coke" spoon. There was a lot of pottery.

In the afternoon, we would have lunch and then head to the rooftop of the museum/house and wash our finds. There were multiple buckets for progressive cleaning, from really, really dirty to cleaner and cleaner, to clean. The best finds went to Madrid. It was a compelling scene, seeing all these people on the roof with their hands in this cold water, concentrating intently, all set in the most beautiful scenery imaginable, looking over the Med. If we were very, very good, Bill would give lectures in the late afternoon on how to reconstruct a pot or vessel from just a fragment. Even the girls were fascinated by how he did this and seeing the enthusiasm in their eyes made me feel vindicated for taking them out of school. They were learning so much.

As the trip went on, we were able to visit the rooms in Valldemossa where Chopin and George Sand spent the winter of 1838—which she recounted not too fondly in "A Winter in Mallorca." We also visited some olive estates and hiked to Soller where we took a trolley and strolled along the port.

My most significant recollection of the trip, however, is distinctly non-archeological. Jackie approached me one day and told me that I had to buy some small gifts for the girls. So, Paula and I, not knowing what this was for, got them a small box of chocolates each. We did not know that in Deya Epiphany is *a*, if not *the*, really big celebration. That evening all of us congregated outside of the village church. The excitement was palpable. Then, from three distinct points across the valley you could see torch lit processions advancing toward us, slowly, with singing.

Gradually, each procession reached the church, being led by someone dressed dramatically as one of the Magi. Processing in, each of the Magi went to the front of the church and the rest of the crowd all followed. Then, having a name of every child in the village, one of the Magi would call their name and the child would run up to the front of the church to receive their gift. Our girls kept looking at us. Anxious to be included, anxious not to be. Not getting their hopes up to be disappointed. Then, amazingly, their names were called. Oh, joy! They both ran to the front of the church to receive huge packages—Jackie had taken the chocolates and wrapped them in enormous boxes for them. Their smiles replaced their faces.

I have subsequently learned that Dr. Waldren passed away in 2003. I tried to write a letter to his family to tell them what a sterling fellow he was and how this trip was so significant to our family. The email came back, but some of our experiences that holiday will be with all of us forever.

Archaeology Definition:

Archaeology is the peeping Tom of the sciences. It is the sandbox of men who care not where they are going; they merely want to know where everyone else has been.

Jim Bishop

22 April 2009

> *"My boyfriend used to ask his mother, 'How can I find the right woman for me?' and she would answer, 'Don't worry about finding the right woman—concentrate on becoming the right man.'"*
>
> Unknown

Dear Dinah,

Since I thought you might need a belly laugh, I though I would talk about some my romantic successes. As you know, in high school, Tina was my girlfriend but that was through no effort on my part. I was so shy and intimidated by girls at that phase that she later told me that if she hadn't asked me out that we never would have gone out.

In college, after some of the other stories that I have mentioned to you, I ended up with Sarah from West Palm Beach. We dated for almost all of my sophomore year. I truly adored Sarah. And, her mother. And, her father. When I visited her down in Florida I remember thinking that I was in heaven, listening to "The Cars" on the radio, cruising with my blond Jewish goddess—because Sarah was most definitely not a Jewish American Princess—and just raising hell. Even her grandmother babied me and brought me "bubkas," little pastries every morning when I was there. It was just like in the dorms when I would return from studying and Sarah would cook pizza bagels on our micro grill. She cooked more for me in those 7 months than Paula has in 25 years. No criticism, just fact.

Even after we broke up it was like, "I know this is strange, but can I still call and talk to "the rents?" I experience the same thing now, from the other side of the fence. Sometimes the girls bring home a guy who I really like and then he is gone. I feel like Rodney King all over again—"can't we just be friends?" Also, Sarah taught me my favorite Jewish expression—it's a double mitzvah on Shabbat (you get double blessing when you do it on holy days). I was multiply blessed.

My troika would not be complete without mentioning Voldemort—or, maybe I should feminize that to Voldermorta, the girl I dated in medical school my freshman year. I must have had a thing for Jewish women—probably still do, but we won't tell Paula—and Va (Voldermorta) was exceptional. Strikingly attractive, intelligent, spoke multiple languages. However, she was a Sabra. Truly, at the risk of generalizing I think that people who grow up under the shadow of total annihilation just do not view the future the same way as others. I really cared for Va, but she was most definitely not into long-term commitments. But, then again, it might just have been me. Probably was.

One Friday night, I thought that it would be quite romantic to have a party for two back in my (crappy) apartment. I bought champagne and deserts and other treats and had music all picked out. I asked Va to come back with me and she just said, "No, I want to see people tonight. Simply not happening." I think that you can see that there was a great deal of self-deception on my part in this relationship!

My most treasured moment, though, was after we returned from a trip to Las Vegas. She had found some trip when we could listen to some real estate pitch for a while and then do shows, dinners and gambling. I paid incidentals. Well, in Chicago on our return I had the cab stop at her place first on the way back. I said, "I will give you a call." To which she replied, "No, I never want to see you again."

Strangely, I think I would have done better had I been gay. I know that I left for college terribly naïve and didn't know much about what put the world around—in those days not everything was quite so supersaturated with sex as not. I remember being so perplexed when I had my freshman English class right after lunch. I would use the lavatory in the English department and got the funniest feelings. All these guys were just so friendly. Finally, I asked one of my roommates about it and he said, "Jesus, you are dumb. Everyone knows that is the gay bathroom. Use the one in the Econ department!"

When I was taking medical Spanish lessons in San Miguel de Allende one year, Paula and I were circumlocuting the central square one morning. She was window shopping and I was—typically—looking at all the people, nurturing my natural inquisitiveness. Suddenly, a really handsome, cute Mexican boy around 25 jumps up and looking right at me yells, "Hola!" Well, I knew what that was about and didn't want to encourage him so I turned and walked on. Paula looked at me and cracked up. For the rest of the trip she would say, "Are you going to go have coffee with Mr. Hola today?"

Perhaps more fun was when we were in the Grand Bazaar in Istanbul. Paula and I were looking at trinkets and not really planning on spending much. However, I passed one booth where they had some fake Dolce and Gabbana belts, with a big D&G on the buckle. Cecily is totally addicted to D&G—she will just say, "Dolce, Dolce, Dolce!"—so I had to look at this stuff. I went into the shop and was browsing when the shopkeeper, a large rather portly Turkish guy came up and started assisting me. Paula was watching his friends who were just laughing at this point. The shopkeeper looked at me and said without warning, "Today is my birthday and I am going to give myself a birthday present." With that, he reached out and enveloped me in the biggest bear hug I have had in ages. So, he got his birthday present. And, I got a very good discount on a D&G belt for Cecily. I did inform her what the actual cost of the belt was.

All joking aside, however, I do think that there are certain looks that play better in certain countries. Americans like big. Big men do much better in this country. This country prefers football, big game, big cars, everything big. Meanwhile, I have done quite well in France. I remember one day in particular. Paula and I were walking around the Palais Royal, I was just wearing a blue Burberry overcoat, and it seemed that every woman who we passed looked at me. I don't know why but that it was a very good day for Steve. Don't have many of those! Maybe that is why I remember it so distinctly. But, I also remember that it was in France, not the U.S. I have never had a day like that in my own country. So, you know what I say to that? Vive la France! Jefferson said that every man has two countries, his own and France. Certainly, that works for me.

> *"Why can't they have gay people in the army? Personally, I think they are just afraid of a thousand guys with M16s going, "Who'd you call a faggot?""*
>
> Jon Stewart

April 23, 2009

> *In each human heart are a tiger, a pig, an ass and a nightingale. Diversity of character is due to their unequal activity.*
>
> *Ambrose Bierce*

Dear Dinah,

We live in the "Gaffney Historic District." At least, that is what one of the former residents here used to call it. I consider that appellation just a might bit presumptuous for our neighborhood—not that I don't like where we live—but Charleston, it ain't. The town is historic, being established in the early part of the 19th century by an Irish tavern keeper. Looking back on it, it seems appropriate that out of all of the cities in the U.S., I would pick one like that.

From a scenic perspective, we have something that I would love to share with you. It is called the Peachoid. It is a giant water tower which is in the shape of a peach. The Peachoid is world famous according to the town's webpage, but perhaps not for the reasons that they desire. The cleft of the peach faces I-85 and before the peach was repainted, it had burnished down to a very human skin tone. Therefore, rather than looking like a peach, it looked more like a butt. Add to this the fact that there is a "dimple" like those, which peaches have on their bottoms, which on our peach looked more like a dingle berry. Now, you can imagine why Gaffney has such a notorious water tower. I rather like it.

We have a very pretty little college, Limestone College, at the end—surprisingly—of College Drive. I like to go running along College Drive, past Oakland Cemetery. When the girls were little, we would take evening walks through the cemetery to see who could find the oldest grave marker. I believe that Paula was the best detective but Cecily did best at raising the dead. I had to confine myself to running along college drive because some people had dogs on some of the side streets and I had several close encounters of the dog kind—not to my liking.

The woman I mentioned, who glamorized our little town as the Historic District, was once married to an attorney. I believe that this was an example of form superseding function, in that outward appearances were quite important but the essence of southern gentility was lacking at times. Sometimes, Cecily would go to play with the daughter and they would just not answer the door—I remember the crestfallen look on her face when she would come back, saying that "the car is there, they just don't answer the door."

In addition, Paula—as you may know by now—is strikingly independent. She doesn't always want to do things like play bridge and "waste time." Marching to her own drummer, she would much rather hole up in bed and read Balzac, or now, I think Dostoyevsky is her preferred poison. So, when she told the lady in question that she would just have to drop out of her bridge club, I knew that a unilateral catfight would happen.

As it turned out, a simple word was all it took. The lady in question told our best friend that we had a rifle in our house that we let the children play with. Actually, I have no guns but I did have a B-B gun that I used—in distant times (beyond the statute of limitations, since Gaffney is a bird sanctuary) to try to make the pigeons stop shitting on our roof. We have a dormer and they loved to live up there and I could not eradicate them. I tried rubber snakes which only decorated the roof, so I had pigeons and rubber snakes. I had fake owls and they sat on them. I read that they didn't like mothballs and tried that, but that just make it smell like you were entering a dry cleaning shop when you came up to our front door. Finally, I capitulated and just had the dormer boxed out. Ha! It did take some convincing to assure the other mother that in fact we did not let the little ones run around with loaded firearms.

Unsurprisingly, the woman who ratted Paula out lived in a house that looked like Tara. And, I don't believe that it had been renovated since the civil war either. But, dramatically, there was an entire genealogy of the family painted on one of the rooms off the living room. Or, I should say, as you might suspect, a "partial" genealogy. For, you see, one day in Spartanburg court was in session and a young (black) vixen was on the stand, giving testimony and the beans sort of got spilled that she had was involved with said Gaffney attorney. And there were some other nefarious financial agreements and quick as a wink the court room was locked and everything on that was sealed. However, it did sort of end his quest to become a judge. I did ask Paula later if his other children would be invited to the birthday parties for the daughter in the big house and she sort of winced. And, laughed. I think we knew the answer.

I must contrast this family to another, one of our closest friends. Their daughter came in the pregnancy way by a none-too-upstanding black guy in the community. However, the result was decidedly different. After the baby was born, the entire family came together as did all of their true friends and I think that this baby is probably just about the most loved, adored and spoiled—in the good way—child in the city. I have no doubt that like Brazilian women of mixed blood she will be an exquisite beauty, as so many children like this are, because already she has me and everyone around her wrapped around all of her little fingers.

It reminds me of an anecdote that I heard, years ago, about a rector at an all girl's school. It was back in the days when it was a family catastrophe that a girl turns up pregnant. He—from what I remember—said that he could tell what the family was like when he called the girl and her parents together and told them about the situation. In the worst cases, the parents would scream, "How could you do this to us?" and the girl would burst into tears, saying, "I never want to see you again." In other cases, the parents would say, "Oh, darling, we are here for you—we will all get through this!" and those girls would invariably say, "Oh, I am so sorry, I love you so much!"

In discussing subjects like this with the nurses at the hospital—I don't know why, but it was always with the nurses that I ended up talking about philosophical issues—they would ask me what I would do if one of my girls was gay or dating a black or non-Caucasian man or went to prison. To me, this always seemed like such a false choice. If they were gay, I don't think that there is much I could do about that. Really, I just don't see that you wake up one day with an attraction to the opposite sex.

And, if they were dating someone—what would be a good turn of phrase here—different? Well, as someone who loves them desperately, I think that I would have to point out that there are narrow minded people in the world and that they might not be choosing the easiest course. Yet, I believe in self-determination and if they feel that they are in love with someone that much, who am I to deny that to them.

Regarding crime and prison, I think personally that would be the most difficult thing for a parent. I think you would have to separate your knowledge of your love for your child from their possible guilt. But, I don't see how—at least in my case—I could ever stop loving my children.

We had a short-term anesthesiologist who worked with us for a while. One day, I asked him if he had children. He said, "Yes." I asked where they lived and he said that one lived in D.C and another lived somewhere in Virginia if I remember correctly. Since he lived in Florida, I said that it must be nice that he was close enough to see them fairly frequently. He said, "No, I don't see them. When their mother and I got divorced and they were 12 and 14, I gave them a choice—they had to choose between her and me and they chose her. So, I cut them off completely then."

Well, several things happened to me at that instant. First, I have never been able to look at that man—let alone think about him—in the same way since. Second, it was like a knife was stuck into my heart! The thought of losing your children over a divorce. I can see wanting a divorce, but my children are such an organic part of me that this is just incomprehensible to me. I would be civil if for no other reason than I adore my children.

Well, that is all from Lake Wobegon, today. Ciao!

What is tolerance?—it is the consequence of humanity. We are all formed of frailty and error; let us pardon reciprocally each other's folly—that is the first law of nature.

Voltaire

24 April 2009

> *"Last night somebody broke into my apartment and replaced everything with exact duplicates . . . When I pointed it out to my roommate, he said, "Do I know you?""*
>
> *Stephen Wright*

Dear Dinah,

I had forgotten how hard it was to move—not having done it in over 20 years! All of the little things to be purchased, new toilet paper, paper towels, Windex. But, at this stage of my life it is easier than when I was younger. At least I do have movers to assist somewhat this time around.

When I first went to college, the difficulty was not the move so much as ending up with a roommate. Freshman year I ended up with a guy from Dallas who played "Mammas, don't let your children grow up to be cowboys," on endless repeat for the entire year. The only thing worse than this was my sophomore year roommate who played Blue Oyster Cult's, "Don't Fear the Reaper," on endless repeat while he did his physical chemistry homework. He should have feared the reaper because I could have throttled him.

Yet, my freshman year roommate was the prize. He was from a more comfortable family than I was, which meant that what was his was his and what was mine was his. For example, if he ran out of soap, he would use mine. But, he had a very nice stereo which I was not permitted to touch. I remember that he went home for Thanksgiving and I stayed in the dorms, not having the money to go home.

He returned unexpectedly early on the following Sunday and—horror of horrors—I was playing a record (if you remember those) on his system. After taking a Quaalude or something, he calmed down enough to take red plastic tape and run it along the floor, up the wall (he didn't go on the window—perhaps, that was just too communal in those liberal times) and along the ceiling and down the back of the door. "You are never to come on this side of the room again."

Except for entering the room—which was somewhat problematic—this did not really redound on me too much. It was somewhat inconvenient for him, though. There was one girl on the floor (in more ways than one) who had worked her way down from seniors, juniors through the sophomores to the freshmen. I took a pass, or actually, didn't. However, he was the last in the chain and hooked up with her. He asked me, "So-and-so and I would like to enjoy ourselves." Wink, wink, nod, nod. I said, go ahead. However, I continued to work at my desk. The two of them left, infuriated and I was rather disappointed that I couldn't offer a running commentary. Alas.

In Chicago, I had my trusty Ford Maverick and had to get a mattress from one place to my new apartment. So, I strapped it to my roof—I imagine that duct tape was involved—and hoped it didn't rain. I do distinctly remember the feeling of vulnerability of hoping the darn thing wouldn't fall off while I was cruising down Lake Shore Drive to the South Side, almost willing through the roof of the car that the mattress would not fall off. I didn't have a Plan B. I wish I had a picture, now.

When we moved to Philadelphia, Paula had preceded me to our apartment. I was finishing my internship and she thought that she would surprise me with the furnishings. However, lacking quality furniture, she elected to "decorate with color." And, decorate she did. When I arrived at our lovely apartment, I felt as if I had entered a fire station or actually, to be more correct, had been plunged into a fire. Paula had painted all of the walls in the living area fire engine red. She was tired and almost tearful—just almost. Yet, she salvaged this mistake, painting one wall yellow and that seemed to cool things down sufficiently. Actually, once she did this it was quite lovely—I know, it doesn't sound it—and we got quite a few compliments. It did start out looking like the Fire Station in Ponce, P.R., though.

When we left Philly, it was wonderful. The military paid for movers. It was like receiving a stimulus check. But, as truth be told, I was wary of a freebie and in this case, appropriately so. The movers were supposed to show up on say a Tuesday at 8 AM and they showed up on a Wednesday at like 6 PM. And, two of the three of them were drunk. Not falling down, droolingly so, but just amusingly so. Like you would enjoy talking with them in a bar but really wouldn't prefer for them to be hauling your furniture—as non-precious as ours was at that particular point in time—into your house. We sent them away after a short while and they finished the job the next day.

After being in D.C. for 4 years, we moved—again, avec movers—to South Carolina. The amazing thing about this move was that we had a little house in Silver Springs chock-a-block with stuff, actually bursting to the seams. We moved into our house in Gaffney and it was like the Hubble effect proving that the universe really is expanding. I think we had something like one or two pieces of furniture in each room. Our house in Gaffney was so big—especially in comparison to where we had been—that we had absolutely nothing to fill it with. In addition, with high ceilings, it seemed even emptier. All of our videos of the girls for the first 10 years show not only the children (and, unfortunately us) aging, but rooms gradually developing character. Hopefully, we have developed character at a faster rate than our rooms.

So, now I am again in transit. The apartment that we have in Wilkes-Barre is absolutely lovely—at least, according to our lights. It is what we like. Old. Hardwood floors. Big windows. There are two baths—thank god—where I can play my "happy morning music" when I get up at 5 AM while Paula lounges until 7—without risk of justifiable homicide on her part. My bath has this funky old green tile and some very retro, art-deco styling. Actually, I feel as if I have stepped back into an Hercule Poiroit movie from the 30's.

And, a personal advantage, from my perspective, is no yard work. I have enough to do, keeping Tara—as I think I will start calling our house in South Carolina—in order. Paula is absolutely insane about roses, so I had a metal plaque made in England, with the words, "Rose Manour." I wanted to put this on our fence, a tongue in cheek comment on her gardening. Yet, she thought this would be a bit too presumptuous for Gaffney. Personally, I thought it was

a) A good joke and

b) I didn't care what people thought.

But, since she refused to mount my little gift on the columns near the gates, I will have to capitulate and satisfy myself with, "Tara." God knows, with that house, there always is another day.

So, erstwhile, I am sitting in a hotel, again waiting for movers. They were supposed to be her Wednesday but confided in Paula (she can extract information from anyone) that they would really be here Thursday. This means that I could have actually stopped in D.C. and gone with Cecily and her friends to "The Flaming Lips" concert. However, I feel somewhat like one of those Christmas snow globes, which you turn upside down to make the snow fall. I am just a bit too agitated at present to enjoy being in Washington right now. I am more comfortable being here just doing the things that I need to do to get ready—getting cable setup Wednesday, finding a gym, all of that stuff. But, the best part of moves at this phase of my life is that I don't have a roommate. Or, if Paula comes up here and puts tape along the ceiling, you will probably next see us on Jerry Springer.

Talk with you tomorrow. You are—as ever—in my prayers.

"Do not spoil what you have by desiring what you have not; remember that what you now have was once among the things you only hoped for."

Epicurus

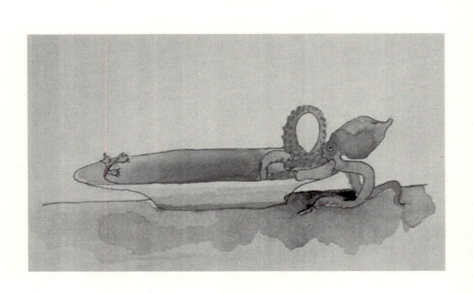

25 April 2009

"Convent: A place of retirement for women who wish for leisure to meditate upon the sin of idleness"

Ambrose Bierce

Dear Dinah,

I don't know about your weather in New York but the weather that I drove into in Wilkes-Barre was cold (by southern standards, at least!), rainy and not happy-happy. I think I will have to go out and buy one of those UV lights to combat depression when I don't see the sun for a while. That might be why—today—we shall travel to the sunny isle of Puerto Rico.

Discussing Puerto Rico with most Americans is enough to drive you crazy. Because, I love the island and its people. But, you would not believe how many times I have entered into conversations with people and the discussion has gone something like this. "Oh, I really don't care for Puerto Rico." "Oh, I love it. Where have you been?" "Well, we got off the cruise ship and spent 4 hours near the port and it just didn't seem that charming." Imagine, getting off of a cruise ship in New York and staying near the port—with some minor allowances—and judging an entire country on that basis!

We went when the girls were young—remembering the photos, I know they were young, but for the life of me, I cannot recall their ages. Ten, twelve? It is funny how when your children are a certain age you can peg the ages of kids in those cohorts but after that they all seem to lose focus. I guess—should I live so long—in about 30 years I will look at old women and be able to tell how old they are based on how old the girls are.

We flew into San Juan and I had researched that we would stay in a building converted from a 350 year old Carmelite monastery into a hotel. The hotel truly was as remarkable as I had anticipated and the location was wonderful—right in the best part of the old part of San Juan. Interestingly, though, we arrived in the midst of one of the worst droughts that the island had experienced in decades. Therefore, the pool water was not sparkling clear but rather a mucky drech such that you could not see the bottom. However, try telling this to kids that need to be fatigued so that the parents can go out later in the evening. Thus, Carter, Cecily and I ended up swimming for hours in this fibringeneous material—obviously, though, without ill effect.

Tourist things aside, like the massive fort El Moro—where the girls tired themselves running about—I have two distinct memories of walking around the city. First, we had stupendous pastries. The food was uniformly good, but the baking was out of this world. And, like all cities, especially hot, packed, summer cities, we would walk out of a café with our pastries and pass an alley and get a jet blast of some absolutely nauseating smell. I have smelled this strange admixture in other places but never quite as distinctly as in San Juan. Now, I must go to Mumbai because I am sure that it can trump anything!

The other thing that I remember about San Juan was the Iglesia de San José (San José Church). I wanted to go here because the section erected in 1532, the main chapel, is supposed to be an excellent example of 16th century Spanish Gothic architecture. And, Ponce de León, was buried here for 300 years until his body was moved to the San Juan Cathedral in 1913. But, as these things turn out, the day we went by to look about, there was a magnificent wedding that was underway. As it turned out, however, this was more special than seeing some dry architecture. All of the tourists and passerby's congregated to look on, the bridal party emerged and the bride had a completely over-the-top, wedding dress. The gaiety and happiness of everyone in the crowd was self-evident with loud cheers. I still have many pictures of this happy couple in our photo albums.

After San Juan, we went along the east coast of the island by car. We stopped in El Yunque National Rain Forest. Let me advise you—never, never, never plan a hike in this rainforest on a Sunday. I believe that every single car from the city had made its journey to the park, every mamacita and papacita and all the children and grandparents, you name it—the entire forest was crawling with not wildlife but happy camping families. But, hiking was brought to a crawl. When I return I shall most decidedly do so on a weekday!

Wending our way along the coast, we started our exploration of paradores. I believe the concept originated in Spain, but Puerto Rico has its own share—unique places to stay, not nameless, shapeless hotels. We stayed in our first one in Yabucoa, along the east coast. The waves were tremendous but the wind was warm and inviting. As it turned out, we met some Italian allergists from Hopkins who were doing the same thing that we were. This was also the first place that Cecily ever had octopus—soon to be her favorite dish. After this, she ate nothing else for weeks. In fact, even on our return to the states we were in International Falls, MN at a diner for breakfast and Cecily ordered octopus. You should have seen the look on the waitress' face.

Leaving the coast, we went inland to a place called Jayuya. First, I must say that Puerto Rico strikes me—in the interior—as a vegetated Switzerland. It has large green mountains, something that I had not anticipated. Second, as we left the major roads to look for Jayuya we ended up on hairpin turns. This made Cecily turn green and she ended up either puking or trying not to for a few hours. The problem was, was that we were committed. So, it was to drive a bit faster and get there sooner or prolong the torture. I need a Bush administration memo on this.

In Jayuya, the girls and two kids from Puerto Rico spent the evening chasing Coquís, a tree frog that puts out and incessant din that I will not even try to describe. Paula and I were more indolent, spending the evening on the veranda with the children's parents, savoring the cool breeze and magnificent tree canopy. If you can pry yourself from the beach, this is a treat on the island.

From Jayuya, we went to Ponce—city of the most remarkable firehouse which I have ever seen—totally red and black. Moving on, we ended up at a resort in Mayagüez for a couple of days before we got a plane and flew off island to Vieques. It is a sad story to recount, but there used to be a resort called La Casa del Frances. A guy named Irving (I think Goldblatt) owned it he was from Boston.

Originally, the hotel had been a banana plantation owned—surprisingly—by a Frenchman. It was a mansion with high ceilings, with slow turning fans and wide verandahs. In all of my research, it appeared that it was one of the last unspoiled island retreats devoted to a laid back, unhurried lifestyle in the Caribbean.

In those days, Vieques was still controlled by the U.S. military and those beaches were pristine and basically empty. We would get a 4 wheeler and go to the beach after coffee in the morning. The beaches were unspoiled, there never would be anyone on them. We would play in the surf and then return to the Casa for lunch. Lounging by the pool, the girls would swim and Paula and I would read—actually, I would snooze. Then, in the late afternoon, we would play combat Scrabble until anger and frustration over Paula always winning would force (me) to quit. Then, we would locate a restaurant for the evening, Cecily getting her obligatory octopus prepared to her liking.

As the girls would say, "our most specialists moment" on the island was swimming the phosphorescent bay. This is a bay choc-a-block with bioluminescent diatoms. When you disturb them, they emit light. There is a bay like this on the main island of Puerto Rico, but petroleum byproducts from engines have degraded its quality. On Vieques, only electrical engines are allowed. We went out on a cloudless, moonless night and were able—under the guidance of our guides—to dive off the boat. Every time you would dive off the boat, you would spread your arms or kick your legs and you would look like an ethereal specter in the water. It was one of the most miraculous things I have ever done.

After a week on Vieques, it was—sadly—back to civilization. However, my memories of Puerto Rico remain strong even at least a decade after our visit there. And, I know another thing. Never to judge a country by a passing glimpse from a stop on a cruise.

> *A cruise on the big new ships is primarily what people want to buy. People are clearly voting with their wallets. We would be very happy to operate smaller ships if they could generate greater profitability than the big ships, but they don't."*

Adam Goldstein

26 April 2009

> *"The cradle rocks above an abyss, and common sense tells us that our existence is but a brief crack of light between two eternities of darkness."*
>
> *Vladimir Nabokov*

Dear Dinah,

This morning I am looking into new beginnings. I am sitting on a yellow plastic carton on my new sun porch in my otherwise completely empty apartment. Sun is streaming into the room—something that I am starting to appreciate might be a rare phenomenon in northeastern Pennsylvania; at least compared to South Carolina! And, I await, expectantly, "the cable man." Or, to give him his druthers, the cable/DSL man.

I have had such a mixture of emotions in the past few months. Happiness at the changes in my life, yet fears about change all the same. And, then to put it into perspective all I have to do is think about you, my dear friend. You are doing so well but have been through such a major event. And, no matter how quickly you mend, it never seems quick enough—save later, in the retrospectoscope.

Heretofore, I have been fairly healthy—but, as we both know that can change for any of us on an instantaneous basis. I live on a day-to-day accounting method. Last night at dinner, with some of my new colleagues, we were discussing one of the surgeons here in the region who had developed laparoscopic cholecystectomies in the area. He had a cardiac arrest outside of Talbot's—I am sure dutifully accompanying one of his women—and is doing quite poorly. The poor guy is in his 70's and we all remarked how young that is. Seventy and young! You and I, Dinah, have come a long way from Albuquerque when we can consider someone in their 70's to be young. And, that number continues to rise, does it not?

Yet, some people—unfortunately, perhaps, not you and I—seem impervious to the dangers of life. One night, when I was on call in South Carolina we received a very large (I mean very large, muscular, built like a Sherman tank) bald black man who had been shot in the belly. He was sitting up quite stoically and was very polite. We needed to explore his abdomen to see what damage had occurred, so I asked him all of the appropriate questions and consented him for anesthesia. He knew that he was going to the operating room. At the conclusion of our little talk he looked at me and very earnestly said, "May I have an aspirin?" I asked him why and he said, "My stomach hurts."

Another night, we received two people who were both shot—a young woman who had several shots into her abdomen and was hemodynamically unstable and a young man who was quite physiologically stable, with only one shot to the abdomen. Now, I would never minimize the placement of exogenous lead anywhere in your body, but I can tell you who I would have though would have done better. But, to everyone's surprise, the young girl did well, with just some minor blood loss and no major damage. However, her boyfriend did not fare so well. He had—as it turned out—been shot in the inferior vena cava, the major difficult vessel to control and try as the surgeons might, they could never control the vessel which had been turned into hamburger.

Unlike you and Paula, I have not had such major encounters with the healthcare system. I do remember as a child seeing a wonderful female pediatrician who I loved very much. She I loved. However, her nurse I hated. And, I mean that. Because after every examination my dear doctor would say, "Mrs. X. is here now," and then the nurse would walk in with her hands behind her back. I always knew what was coming—a shot. She would lie to me and say, "No, it is just a bee." I was a holy terror I am sure, but I knew that was no fricking bee.

I did not get better with age. When I went to Honduras with Interplast I had to get shots. I went to one of my local doctor friends to get the full complement and one—because of the short time involved—was the Hepatitis A injection. I remember distinctly shouting and they laughed. The patients in the waiting room asked if someone was hurt and they said, "No, that is just a doctor getting a shot." Everyone was quite amused. Save me.

One thing—and, I guess probably the only thing—I have really learned and internalized in life is not to try to do "what the big kids do." Maybe this would have helped Bernie Maddof's investors? Over on Spring Avenue, we used to play by the freeway. To this day I do not know who came up with the idea of doing it, but it was a highly respected "big kid." They had a red wagon and said, "Why don't we ride the wagon down the side of the hill next to the freeway? Volunteers?"

Well, Butthead here either volunteered or was selected and ended up riding that wagon down the hill. This might have gone fine, save for one minor problem. There was a telephone pole at the bottom of the hill. So, in this case, nose met telephone pole. Telephone pole won and nose got flat. Thus began my experience of ENT surgeons.

First, I just when home and climbed into bed because I knew that I was in trouble for being so stupid. I wasn't—one look from my parents and I knew I was forgiven by the horrified look on their faces, as if that was a consolation. The ENT surgeon that night just manipulated my nose, sans anesthesia. Enough said on that one.

Later, after my senior year of high school, I had to have a nose job—or, shall we say, corrective rhinoplasty. This was to get me back to what God had intended and end the "Evil Kanasal" moniker which I had acquired. Now, subliminally there might be a reason for this in my choice of specialties, anesthesia, but my ENT then did his cases under local. I think that you would be put in prison for this now but they held me down and stuck needles in my nose for "local anesthesia." Then, I heard all of the chipping and hammering for what seemed like ever. And, felt the big, hairy arms of the female nurse restraining me.

They must not have known much about swelling then, either, because my nose swelled up like a hog's and you could look straight into my nostrils. I was quite fetching. I looked so bad that Mom and Dad put paper over the mirror in my room so I wouldn't get too depressed. Also, because of the stress my sclera all bruised and turned red at first. However, as the hemoglobin was reabsorbed I ended up with a rainbow coalition of colors in the whites of my eyes.

Finally, I couldn't take it anymore and too this day I remember my first soirée out of the house. I went to the McDonalds near Manzano and was sitting there eating a cheeseburger, sipping a coke. A little 5 year old boy came over near me and started staring. I looked at him and smiled. Looking back at me, he threw back his head, screamed and ran off. I don't know whether it was my pig nose of black eyes that did it.

Maybe it is an ENT thing in our family. I know that Cecily had to have her tonsils removed when she was in college. We scheduled it when she was home over break and one of my good friends did her surgery. However, doing procedures on friends is always a risk—you get such "better" care than regular patients. Cecily re-bled from her tonsil and I had to call his Dad a few days later to look at her (he is also an ENT). His Dad is a phenomenal surgeon, having saved mom's jaw when she had oral cancer. So, when he told me he thought that he could cauterize the "small bleeder" in the holding room without going to the OR, I was all in favor of that.

For anesthesiologists, bleeding tonsils have their own risks and you prefer to avoid putting people to sleep with blood in their stomachs. You don't want them to vomit that blood into their lungs, causing an aspiration. Yet, I don't think that he, and I most definitely know that I didn't think that the holding room would turn into a mini-operating room in its own right. Poor Cecily. She ended up with several shots and much cautery. Because of me, her Dad the anesthesiologist, she ended up with inferior care and virtually no anesthesia.

Dinah, I hope this letter finds you doing Sunday New York Times crossword puzzles. And, if not that, crosswords from perhaps the Albuquerque Tribune. Save that, maybe a Sudoku or two? And, if not that, sitting in the sun like a big fat lazy cat enjoying the day. Because, in point of fact, all of us have a limited number of days and it is the blessings you bring to others that count. And, you have added to my life in so many ways that you will probably never know them all.

Bis spatter!

"Surgery is by far the worst snob among the handicrafts"

Austin O'Malley

27 April 2007

> *"Old age has been charged with being insensible to pleasure and to enjoyments arising from the gratification of the senses, a most blessed and heavenly effect, truly, if it eases us of what in youth was the sorest plague of life"*
>
> Marcus Tullius Cicero

Dear Dinah,

I was delighted to receive your email today! I am glad that you are doing so well. I never suspected less from you. Yet, if you are driving I know that you are firmly back with us. However, without being too ironically cruel, having dealt with Libby and also having had to take away Mom's car, I do have a feel for who the will let on the roads. I love you enough not to classify you in that group!

Before I get underway with any particular topic today, I have to let you know about the latest news from Lucy. Apparently—God knows where this has come from—Paula and Lucy were having coffee with Mom yesterday and Mom started going on and on about how much I look like Lucy's daughter, Miranda. As Carter would say, "this is just wrong on so many levels." First, Miranda is just about the prettiest girl around, with luminous dark eyes, a fetching smile and luxuriant hair. I am—well, a middle-aged guy fighting off that stuff around the middle with graying hair. And, being needlessly explicit, Miranda has beautiful coffee-colored skin and I am pasty white, not tanning too well.

So, there they were and Lucy initiates the attempt—perhaps Mom meant Cecily or Carter. "Mrs. Boggs," because Lucy always calls Mom "Mrs. Boggs, don't you mean Carter or Cecily?" The answer was an emphatic, "No." "No, I think that Miranda looks just like Steven." Paula tried—although what other tacks she could have attempted just baffle me, but try she must. Ultimately, the battle was conceded. Miranda and Steven look just alike. Poor Miranda. Please, put her in your prayers.

This is only slightly analogous to the time that the girls had some friends in town from college and we all went to dinner—Carter had a boyfriend from UVA and Cecily had a guy friend from Spartanburg. So, there we are at the local Mexican restaurant eating and Paula was waxing on one of her favorite topics, familial inheritances. So, she is saying how

Carter looks like me but acts like her and how Cecily looks like a Johnson but acts like me. But, then she added, "But Cecily is just like Steve from the waist down." Well, you have known me long enough to know that I could not allow this to pass. So, I said, deadpan, "Well, except for the penis." The boys looked down at the table and then at the girls and then finally at me. Then, explosively, everyone burst into laughter. So, our standing joke in the family is still that Cecily and I look alike from the waist down.

Unfortunately, I probably have only one more week of "good writing" left, before I start my new job up here in Pennsylvania. Yesterday, the movers arrived and delivered the packages. In less than 24 hours, I have unpacked every box. I just couldn't sleep with stuff not put away. However, it was hard to sleep; not because I hadn't put stuff away, which I had. Rather, because every fiber in my body ached last night. I was in such pain that I couldn't move. But, today was better. And, I am free tomorrow before I fly to Mississippi for one last week.

I will continue to write, albeit at less of a breakneck pace, once I start work. Yet, tonight I wanted to discuss something near and dear to my heart. On April 21st of this year I celebrated my 9th year of sobriety, entering gladly into my 10th year of recovery. This has been the most profound journey that I have ever taken. Just to give you some background, drinking alcoholically makes you do things that you would look down on, that you would never ordinarily do. I know that happened to me. Fortunately, my run was not particularly long and did not end tragically for me or for another.

On the night of April 20th, which happened to be a Maundy Thursday, I finished drinking at my favorite watering hole and was picked up for a DUI near my house. When the officer asked me to do a field sobriety test I asked if I had to take both hands off the trunk of my car. The next thing I remember saying was, "Those handcuffs are rather tight." So, I had a glamorous night in the Cherokee County jail—with a young black fellow also in for DUI, who seemed normal like me—for those of us cognoscenti—and then another truly bizarre young black guy, who paced the whole night and was totally freaked out. He was in for trespassing. The first guy and I sort of made a tacit agreement to watch out for Mr. Bizarro.

Leaving jail the next day, Good Friday, Paula and I met with a counselor and I agreed to go to Talbot in Atlanta. My referring doctor said that he wanted to "maximize my "dose" for recovery." I thought that I was going for 2 weeks and was there for 4 months. I can, without any reservation, say that this was the most transformative experience of my life. When I went to treatment I thought that I could not live without alcohol. Talbot did not teach me—completely—that I could, but they gave me the tools to continue to work toward a life of sobriety.

Sobriety is such a misunderstood concept. For those of us who drink alcoholically, to be sober is not merely to learn how to live without alcohol but also to learn to live happily without alcohol, to learn to cope with the vagaries of life in a more normal manner and to learn that life will go on. Frequently, I am asked how I know that I am an alcoholic. Well, in my case I use an illustration. When most people drink, after a few glasses of wine or some mixed drinks, a flashing red light goes off in their heads. This does not happen in my case. Rather, after a few glasses of wine, a flashing green light goes off in my head and a neon arrow points, saying, "This is where the conga line starts!"

After Talbot—which would be a book in its own right, perhaps one I should write—I returned to Gaffney and took a few months off before returning to work. It was wonderful because it was in the fall. In the South, the girls' tennis season is in the fall and the boys have the spring. That way, there is court time for everyone. So, I was able to attend every single practice that the girls had. Not just games, mind you, but practice. It was intoxicating, in a totally different way. The leaves were changing, the air would be warm and turn brisk as the evening dragged on. And, I had a very good chance to experience time with my daughters that I had not been able to enjoy because I had worked so many hours previously.

The man whom I am closest to, whom I depend in to a large degree in my recovery, is a Harley riding pony-tailed man, half-Irish, half-American Indian. He told me, "Steve, I didn't have a chance." And, like this guy, looking back at my genetic history I see that there were "influences," to be generous. My genetic father was a belligerent alcoholic. And, I have a half-sister who had some trouble with cocaine. So, late in life I am not surprised that I found alcohol.

The first time ever that I drank was on my People-to-People trip to Europe after my junior year of high school. I remember distinctly being in Holland and drinking 18 Heinekens. And, I was proud of that. Only now, do I recognize that tolerance is a hallmark of a potential alcoholic. Moreover, why did I like it so much? Because I never felt good in my own skin. I was an anxious, neurotic teenager. And, they always say that you stop developing emotionally when you start drinking. So, I still have quite a bit of developmental delay by that calculus!

The past 9 years have been the best years of my life, despite my ups and downs. And, I have not felt the urge to drink despite having dealt with two teenage daughters, getting them through high school and college. I thank God that I was in recovery so that I was able to support Paula when she had her breast cancer diagnosis. And, I have been a much better son for Mom through all of this. That is not bragging. I know how bad a son I would have been if I had been drinking, I am only making a comparison.

I have specifically not tried to innumerate the outrageous things I did "back in the day" in this letter. Like the time in D.C. when I—who knows where these ideas come from in the mind of an alcoholic—that we were in a bar with large posters of famous movies stars on the walls. For some reason, the idea came into my head to buy a pack of cigarettes and also chewing gum. I proceeded to go from one poster to the next, chewing a piece of gum, then lighting a cigarette and then sticking it on the poster—so that the star would have a lighted cigarette. I think I got them all that night. Yes, I could go on and on about that type of thing.

Some are funny. Some aren't. However, like I tell people whom I talk to who are trying to stop drinking, we all drink or drank because we liked the feeling. Simple. There was always an excuse. "I had a good day." "I had a bad day." "I am celebrating." "I am depressed." "I work too hard." Yet, when I drink it is not like going back to when I was 18 again. I will never be able to drink that way again. Rather, I drink compulsively. Therefore, for me it is better just not to take that first drink.

To tell you how screwed up an alcoholic's thinking is, when I got out of treatment I saw a magazine advertisement with a young couple sitting in chairs, looking out over a beach. They had two drinks between them. My first thought was, "Ah, I will never have a good time again." Then, I took a closer look. They were drinking iced tea. It was all in my perception.

I can honestly say that I would not change my course. Before I had to find sobriety, I was too much of a self-satisfied prig. Having a dose of humility has made me a better husband, a better father and I hope a better doctor. I know that it has made me more compassionate to those who graciously allow me to treat them. And, I am a little kinder to myself. Because, much of that drinking was driven by internal struggles. That, however, is fodder for another letter.

> *"Man seeks to escape himself in myth, and does so by any means at his disposal. Drugs, alcohol, or lies. Unable to withdraw into himself, he disguises himself. Lies and inaccuracy give him a few moments of comfort."*
>
> *Jean Cocteau*

28 April 2009

> *"Skiing combines outdoor fun with knocking down trees with your face."*
>
> Dave Barry

Dear Dinah,

    Today driving around Wilkes-Barre, Elton John came on the radio and it took me back to high school when you, Greg and I would go skiing at Sandia. It seems so long ago, Greg being the best skier of the three of us, me jealously trying to keep up with him but not succeeding and you—judiciously coming down the slope, thinking us foolish for being engaged in some sort of testosterone driven competition. Typically, though, the day would finish and for some reason the song that always seemed to be playing on the radio was, "Philadelphia Freedom."

    Another time, when I was home from college, I thought that I would be cool and after skiing all morning, I had a couple of brandies with lunch. That was not smart. Then, I decided to ski down the trail, "Suicide," without preparation. That was even less smart. I might have done it with deliberation or without the brandies, but not with this mixture. I still remember the sort of dazed feeling I had when—after I had fallen and recovered myself—I brushed my glove against my head and quizzically wondered, "What is this red stuff?" The tip of my ski had cut my forehead right above my eyebrow and it was bleeding like stink, like all facial wounds do.

    I waited at the Red Cross hut for a long time and then had to capitulate and take the chairlift up to the top, then take the tram down and then drive down—I went to the American and Dad drove me to Lovelace. There, I just had some stitches. Fortunately, the doc was a skier and we had a nice chat. However, self-pride and not knowing my own limits never did me well. If I had been Columbus, I doubt that the New World would have been discovered. Maybe, just the Azores.

    It is sort of like the comparison that I have heard between Beethoven and Schubert—one inhabits the highest peaks and the lowest depressions, the other dwells in gently sloping valleys. I am the latter, much more suited to the nuances of everyday life.

    When I turned 40 I decided that I needed to have a more major adventure. So, I enrolled with Outward Bound, hiking in the Pisgah

National Forest in North Carolina for 10 days. This was to be a zero-impact hike, so we were to take nothing in that we would leave. We used cook stoves; if you build a fire, you sterilize the ground due to the heat and make that soil useless environmentally for a long time. Therefore, we ate everything, cleaned our pots with leaves, used leaves for toilet functions and basically had low imprint.

The first 5 days of the trip were an absolute washout. That is not hyperbole. It rained for 5 days straight. Every article that I had was wet. No matter what we did, we ate in the rain, hiked in the rain, pooped in the rain, slept (fitfully) in the rain. I have a phenomenal respect for our Marines and others who do stuff like this. It is hard. I am sure that I was absolutely the worst camper. After about day 3 I started whining. But, there was a small Asian girl, a lab technician from Detroit, who was an absolute stoic. She inspired me and kept me going. She kept her head down, never once complained and was a great example. In fact, she and I still keep in touch we became such good friends on this trip.

And, after our proverbial 40 days of rain minus 35, the sun came out and the rest of the trip was one of the best experiences of my life. We rappelled on two days. Other nights I remember sitting with a coach from the Midwest and just staring at panoply of stars—absolutely breathtaking. We both stared with slack-jawed and shocked amazement that there were so many stars in the heavens. The food tasted better, the hiking became so much easier and the camaraderie was wonderful.

I distinctly remember driving home, not having bathed or shaved in almost 2 weeks. I wanted to hug and kiss the girls and they refused to have anything to do with me—until I was properly shaved, showered and dressed. No matter how bad things get politically and economically in this country, I do not think that we will every go back quite to those primitive conditions. Should we ever return to a Thomas Hobbesian State of Nature, what with life being nasty, brutish and short, many of us will be unkissed and unloved.

Speaking of the girls, I cannot help but remember how envious I was of you and Jim when we used to see you up in Hamptons—we would be visiting Gwen and Jordan with the girls and you would be young and without kids. One time, in particular, I remember carting Cecily's playpen to the beach. Most decidedly not Hamptons material, are we. I am sure that the people that really are in the Hamptons have someone to watch their children or—in extremis—they have someone schlep their playpen for them!

But, that does not even begin to compare with the big even that I am sure you have never forgotten. It was so wonderful of you to choose Carter as flower girl for your wedding. I know how excited both Paula and I were over this, yet how we didn't want to go on about it too much because we didn't want Carter to go freaky about having to walk down the isle in front of all of those people. Little did we know that she would rise to the occasion without any problem. Knowing her now, I can only say that stage fright is not one of her issues. She may have issues, but that is not one of them.

She looked so sweet and innocent in her dress and your entire wedding was a dream. I remember your mother looking pretty but more distinctly I remember your father looking very distinguished in his uniform. And, at the reception later—grand and sporty. I am so glad that we were able to stay and enjoy it and that you let us leave Carter in your God-awfully expensive honeymoon suite.

I still recall the panicky feeling that night when Paula and I prepared to leave and we went to retrieve Carter and discovered that she had wet your wedding bed. It is just one of those things that you do not anticipate and Emily Post gives you no guidance. Should you leave a written note? "On the occasion of your nuptials, Paula and I send you golden showers, courtesy of Carter, your flower girl." Would this be better in French? "A l'occasion de votre marriage, Paula, et je vous envoyer des douches d'or, courtesy de Carter, la fleur de votre fille. Or, did we do better as we acted, calling the hotel and emergently trying to towel down everything that we could and then doing a full confession? Je ne sais pas!

So, in a manner of speaking, you and I are bound like I am with my friends Sheila and Tom from my Outward Bound trip. There, we suffered from relentless rain for 5 days and emerged with a stronger friendship for it. You and I started as friends and—with a little extra shower coming into our lives, and the forbearance of your husband—have remained better and better friends. Hopefully, now that you are on the path to recovery, which will be the last wet or cloudy day, you will see for a while.

> *"If I were running the world I would have it rain only between 2 and 5 a.m. Anyone who was out then ought to get wet."*
>
> *William Lyon Phelps*

29 April 2009

> "My whole thesis is that you can't understand America until you understand Appalachia."
>
> Jeff Biggers

Dear Dinah,

    A couple of times we have taken family houseboat vacations. I do not know if you have ever done this, but these are rare events. Living in such tight proximity—even with people with whom you ordinarily share your lives—intensifies everything.

    The first time we did this was just with our nuclear family. We rented a houseboat on "Lake in the Woods," which is on the border between Kentucky and Tennessee. The girls were younger—as I have said, exact ages escape me, but they must have been around 10. We drove up one Saturday and rented the boat for a week.

    I can only say that areas such as this are rather "rural." Once, when Paula and I were living in Chicago we decided to drive down from the city to hike in the Daniel Boone National Forest for a long weekend. So, we drove all day and in the later part of the afternoon finally arrived in our selected city, near the park. We checked in and I can still remember that we didn't take our shoes off—the carpet must have had biologic forms growing in it. I am sure that some of my microbiology professors would have been able to discover new, undescribed forms living there. In addition, we had passed many cars, some on cinderblocks, some not, with curtains in them, where people were living. I truly felt as if I had entered the Appalachia that I had read about. "Let us now Praise Famous Men."

    So, we entered the restaurant and before we ordered we asked the girl/waitress/lady about town for a beer. She said, "I can't do that—this is a dry county." Well, in those days, being from Chicago, this was completely amusing. But, I asked, "How far is the closest place that we can get a beer?" She gave me the name of the place, but added, "You don't want to go over there!" When I asked why not, she said, "Well, it is 15 miles away!" It turns out that in her entire life she had never been "over there," because it was too far away. If she had really, really understood that we had driven from Chicago that day just to hike she probably would have viewed us as space aliens.

We do have people like that is South Carolina. I haven't met any myself but some of my friends who are from Gaffney and some of my doctor friends swear that there are a lot of people in town who have never seen the ocean. I consider that a travesty and a tragedy. Now, I know that growing up in Albuquerque I didn't see the ocean until I was a teenager and we went out to L.A. to Disney Land. But, being from South Carolina, when it is only a few hours drive. Unimaginable.

But, returning to my houseboat story, we moved around the lake slowly. I am at a loss for the best verb to use for a houseboat. We sort of scooted but that seems sort of land-based. Ambled seems too foot-based. Percolated along seems too speedy. In a houseboat you sort of hope that you don't have much current—at least the 3 horsepower boat that we had. We did run aground several times but fortunately we were going so slowly that we didn't hurt either ourselves or our archaic vessel.

The days took on a very pleasant constancy. The girls would swim and use the slide off the back of the boat all morning while Paula and I would sip coffee. Lunch was a very haphazard affair. Afternoons were for sleeping, swimming, fishing. And, I don't know where I got it into my head but I decided that we should have "reading hour" each night—which actually turned into reading 3-hour. I had brought, "Johnny Tremain," a book that I remembered fondly from school. We blasted through that and went on into other books.

More evocative remembrances also come back to me. The toilet on this boat smelled to high heaven after like the first day. None of us could stand sleeping near it. I say that, with the exception of Cecily. For some reason, it was like Morpheus' dreams for her. She could sleep through anything. So, each night, the rest of us would lay in bed, talking, trying to drift off to sleep, but before you could say, "God that stinks," Cecily would be asleep. It was the same thing in the afternoon. I have always said that she is an amazing girl and this is just one aspect of her amazing personality!

I must also confess—as you probably know—that I am a complete failure as a sportsman. I have all the Orvis gear to be a fly fisherman but casting in the North Carolina streams is difficult. I have an uncanny propensity for getting my lines in the most difficult places—and, not where they are supposed to be. Like my neck. Well, on this houseboat trip I tried and tried all week to catch a fish. Any fish. For lures, I tried everything. I tried chicken. I tried worms. I tried early and late in the day. I tried various depths and being noisy and still. You name it.

But, the last day, early in the morning I cast out past a flock of ducks and really got a tug. I started reeling my line in and suddenly there was the most horrific screeching—squawk, squawk, squawk! It appeared that I had hooked a duck. So, I had a difficult choice. I didn't want to cut the line long because that could hurt the duck—it might get tangled in something later. So, I decided to reel it in and cut the line short. By this point the girls and Paula were on deck yelling, "Daddy caught a duck! Daddy caught a duck!" Yeah, Paula, too.

You might survive not being a golfer in the South. And, you might survive not being a great sportsman, too. But, it really does not help when your daughters return from vacation and see an internist friend of yours—who happens to deep sea fish in Costa Rica and hunt in Alaska—and they proudly tell him that when Daddy went fishing in Kentucky he caught a duck. It did something to my reputation that just happens to rhyme with ducked.

The second time we took a houseboat trip was when the girls were in high school. However, this time we went with Paula's sister, Jill, and her family. This time, we had two houseboats and unlike Jill's husband, Jerry, I seemed to find every single rock in the entire Rainey Lake. Jerry was continually pulling me off of rocks. However, he did this rather proudly, smiling knowingly that an avid outdoorsman such as himself would not put himself in such predicaments.

This trip was different. There was little fishing and a lot of reading. My girls were fascinated by their older cousins, Crystal and Sabrina. Therefore, the estrogen horde were groomed, lathered and covered with sun oil on the top of one boat. I—unsuccessfully—tried to recruit Sabrina to help me form the "Jane Austin Fishing Club," but she gave me that look, tragic and pathetic, that only a teenage girl can give to a man who is completely older, pathetic and clueless. Withering might be an apt descriptor.

One night, we found an island with all sorts of posted signs, "Fires in designated areas only." So, we built a fire in a designated area. But, I do admit—in retrospect—that we got a little carried away, probably having found every loose piece of twig, timber, log, you name it and built a blaze that could be seen for miles. I am glad of two things. First that we didn't burn up the whole island. Second, that we were on houseboats and could have floated away if we had succeeded in the former.

Ultimately, this trip, too, came to a conclusion. They say that karma is a bitch and It most certainly felt that way—if only for Jerry that day. He was speeding ahead of us, we laggards—with Jill on our boat—when we heard a phenomenal crack. Jerry had run aground. When we got there, every plate, cup and spoon, simply everything was tossed around the galley. The rest of us laughed until our sides split while Jerry fumed and cursed. I understood perfectly.

"People need trouble—a little frustration to sharpen the spirit on, toughen it. Artists do; I don't mean you need to live in a rat hole or gutter, but you have to learn fortitude, endurance. Only vegetables are happy."

William Faulkner

30 April 2009

> *"I told my psychiatrist that everyone hates me. He said I was being ridiculous—everyone hasn't met me yet."*
>
> Rodney Dangerfield

Dear Dinah,

Anesthesiology is somewhat the Rodney Dangerfield of medical specialties. Obviously, surgery and surgeons get the glamour—if in no one else's eyes but their own. In the old days, internal medicine was purported to be the thinking man (or woman's) specialty. However, with evidenced-based practice and practice guidelines, many office-base practices are so regulated that autonomy as known in the past has long disappeared. Psychiatry sounds interesting but as it is practiced now, very little counseling is done—which is the part that I find of interest. Rather, psychologists and other practice extenders do the counseling and most psychiatrists dispense medication. I could go on and on.

In college, I started as a philosophy major. I can honestly say that the most difficult course I ever took in my life was symbolic logic. I remember studying modus ponens and modus tollens and that was the very easy, elementary stuff. Then, we got to propositional calculus, set theory, Russell's paradox and some other very esoteric proofs which I found fascinating but exceptionally difficult. I worked my ass of in that course and eked out a B+. With gratitude.

Realizing early on that I would never have what it took to be a tenured philosophy professor, I switched to the School of Engineering, studying electrical engineering. I loved the purity of the mathematics, fields and waves, and the physics. However, computers and I did not really love one another. This was when you had to do your programming with a large packet of punch cards and wait for your set to run at 2 or 3 AM. My impatience and lack of attention to detail did not make me the best computer scientist. I seen now, if I had been able to take it I could have gone to California in the early 80's as a computer scientist and would probably be retired now. Alas.

What got me going was my professors in engineering convinced me that if I had a medical degree and the engineering degree, I would be able to get great grant funding. So, I was a double major in electrical engineering and biology—concentrating on cell biology. I took physical chemistry instead of biological chemistry, thinking that I would get the latter course in medical school. Ultimately, I got mono my senior year and had to drop a couple of electrical engineering courses so I didn't finish with that degree. I can't remember the name of the girl I got that from, but I do remember sleeping a lot.

I say all of this to give you context for how difficult I found my first year of medical school. I was so used to deriving things, not just memorizing things. I would definitely tell a premed student now to take biochem and to take a developmental biology course. I remember my first anatomy course. I walked in and they said, "Mr. Boggs, what is this structure?" I said, "Well, let me check my atlas." "Oh, no, no, no! You must memorize these things!" I did pass that exam—barely. Anatomy and I were never good friends. Biochem and I got along better for at least I could see some reason for the processes there.

Medical school was medical school. Pritzker was very conventional in those days—first year anatomy, biochem, neurobiology and anatomy. Second year pathology and histology. Third year clinical rotations such as surgery, internal medicine, pediatrics, psychiatry, obstetrics, and a few minor electives. Fourth year was primarily elective. I remember that I was gung-ho to be a surgeon, if for no other reason than that is what Mom expected of me. However, my advisor was a world-famous vascular surgeon. We had long talks and I told him that I liked managing very ill patients but really didn't care for the surgery. He told me that I should consider anesthesia.

The chairman of anesthesia at Chicago in those days was a Renaissance guy named Donald Bensen. He had been the first chairman of anesthesia at Hopkins and he took me under his wing. I did a rotation with his people and liked it and decided to pursue anesthesia—I especially loved the physiology and the pharmacology. You could give a drug and see immediately its effect in the body. Because Paula and I were serious by this time, I decided to do a year of internal medicine at Chicago and then do my residency in anesthesia at Penn.

People have such a distorted view of anesthesia—for example that anesthesiologists have no patient contact. Actually, we have a great deal of patient contact. And, it is not easy task to take someone coming in for an operation and with limited time try to dispel their anxiety. Moreover, I have learned—with life-experiences and time—that a case that might be simple from a surgical and anesthetic perspective may have completely different emotional overtones for the patient. Imagine, if you would, trying to alleviate the tremendous fear and upheaval in a woman in the holding room who presents for an excision of a breast mass. The case and anesthetic are relatively minor. However, I can assure you that this is not a minor case for either this woman or her family. I know that, particularly well now, having trod down this path myself. And, that is just one example.

Also, anesthesia has changed significantly since I went into it. In those days we used to do some blocks and general anesthesia. We even told some people—back in those dark ages—that they were too sick to be put to sleep. That has all changed. We basically tackle almost any case, due to improvements in monitoring, pharmacology and anesthetic techniques. In 1984 when I did my first heart it was typically a single or double bypass in a younger male. One week in South Carolina, when I did nothing but hearts for a week, I kept track and didn't do any one younger than 85 years of age and these were all for complicated CABG cases, valves or double valves.

We also are much more concerned with post-operative pain relief than ever before and other things that extend into the post-op period, like glucose regulation.

The biggest challenge that I see for our specialty now is being efficient yet resisting all of the temptations to be cogs on a wheel—sort of like that old "I Love Lucy" episode where she and Ethyl are making chocolates. You can only work so quickly no matter what the process is before the error rate will start to creep up. Management wants complete efficiency, but sometimes talking with a patient, the humane practice of medicine requires that you ignore efficiency and focus on other aspects of medical practice.

We also tend to be the psychologists of the operating room. Twenty years ago when I started in Spartanburg, I was working with my favorite cardiac surgeon—who remains one of my best friends. However, like every relationship you have your ups and downs. He always wanted the blood pressure to be 90/60 for his carotid endarterectomies. Well, as you can imagine, with various degrees of stimulation and other factors, the blood pressure may run around that number but will not always be exactly there—no matter how good you are. So, every time he looked up, the pressure would be 110/70 or perhaps 80/50. Not terrible, but something I would be working on. And, every time he would look up, it would be one of these other figures, not the 90/60 which I generally had.

Finally, in utter exasperation he looked at me and said, "I want that pressure to be 90/60." So, in utter exasperation myself, I took a 3 x 5 index card and wrote, 90/60 on it in big block letters. I taped this up on the monitors so that I could see the actual pressure and he could only see the index card. The next time he looked up he said, "What is the pressure?" I said, "It is always 90/60 because that is what you want it to be." We had no problems after that and after that he concentrated on his job and let me do mine. And, he is the best heart surgeon I have worked with.

"I'm at the age where food has taken the place of sex in my life. In fact, I've just had a mirror put over my kitchen table."

Rodney Dangerfield

1 May 2009

"Quite frankly, teachers are the only profession that teach our children."

Dan Quayle

(Dan Quayle is Chairman of an international division of <u>Cerberus Capital Management</u>, a multi-billion dollar <u>private equity</u>—with guys like this in private equity, could this explain the economy?)

Dear Dinah,

Strangely, for some reason, I have been thinking of friends of mine who have been teachers. I don't think that it has anything with it being the first of May; usually I associate school with autumn. All those years in the educational system and I associate dying leaves with new beginnings. But, ah, I did love the smell of newly sharpened pencils and the opportunity to go and buy new notebooks. May, for me on the other hand, represented "the end of everything I loved." As an only child, it represented the prospect of a long, bleak, lonely summer by myself, since generally I didn't have camp to look forward to.

The only camps I could ever afford to go to were Boy Scout camps, and I was an absolute failure as a boy scout. That is somewhat of a non sequitur, but I do promise to get back to the teachers. As a cub scout—there I was excellent. I must have had 40 zillion little project badges on my insignia as a Webelo. So, I assumed that I would easily get by as a boy scout. Au contraire! What held me up was the swimming. I made it easily to second class. However, I could not get beyond that because to get into first class you had to swim a certain distance in a lake. This just terrified me. I couldn't see the bottom. I know that you can drown in a cup of water and I had been swimming in the "deep end" of a pool for years. But, this psychological barrier was just too much. I tried to negotiate with the counselors: "Could I do this distance in a pool?" "No, it must be in a lake." I was wasting my time. So, my Boy Scout career ended at a very prematurely developed stage as a second class.

One summer, Dad actually got away from Guard duty and came up to teach wilderness navigation with the Boy Scouts. I was so thrilled and excited. I was exceptionally proud of the fact that he would be there and even more excited at the prospect of spending some time with him.

Unfortunately, I had not banked on also being an abysmal failure at wilderness navigation. Give me a compass, a heading and a map and you could pretty much guarantee that I would

a) Not ever end up where you wanted me to be, and

b) That I would be the last to ever find his way back to camp.

Compounding my disappointment—Dad found a kid who was sharp as a tack in tracking and all this stuff and really took him under his wing. My failures were compounded before my eyes as Dad became this boy's private coach. The entire experience was humiliating.

The third thing that made me realize that I had no potential to be an outdoorsman in those days was that I used to sleepwalk. It was bad enough at the house, when a couple of times I was rescued from peeing on the coats in the front hall closet, because I thought that I was in the bathroom—or, when I was about to take excursions outside. But, you can imagine how thrilling it was for me, on more than one occasion, to wake up at 3 in the morning, standing on a log, God knows where, in the middle of the forest. Usually, I hadn't gone far, but it usually did take a while for my eyes to acclimate to the darkness so that I could figure out where I was. It was also quite "fun" almost crawling into the wrong sleeping bag, i.e. with someone in it, in the night. Fortunately, my pre-pubescent development saved me from other accusations there.

But, returning to teachers. Over the years I have loved their stories as they have loved some of my medical anecdotes. As far back as when Paula and I first got married, my cousin's wife, Melinda, used to teach in the Wilmington, Delaware public schools. She would regale us for hours with stuff the kids would do. My favorite was the "collection." Over the years, Melinda had amassed a collection of notes which she had confiscated from her students. Some were tragically amusing. One, between two girls, talked about how they were vying for the attentions of one of their uncles. "He be coming to my house for his birthday present and I am going to give him a big present." Then, the other girl had written below more dialogue about what she was going to do to this guy for his birthday. This went through several stanzas—almost like a pornographic Elizabethan love sonnet, albeit less articulate but a great deal more graphic. Were they not so young (but, surely not inexperienced), a man could not help but envy this "lucky uncle." Lolita in Wilmington.

In Gaffney, one of the women who goes to our church has taught for over 20 years, variously grades 3 to 5. She says that she reads the local paper and peruses it to see who has committed the rapes, burglaries and murders.

Invariably, with her long track record in the community, she has taught most everyone and she swears that she can tell you, "I could have told you when they were in 3rd grade that they would end up like that."

Another friend of ours, another teacher in our church, teaches high school. My favorite Kim story is about the young boy who fell in love with her when she had him for 10th grade. He fancied himself cool, quite a lothario. Frequently, he offered to do anything for her. The day that it was all brought to a head was one day when she had to reach overhead to work the television—so that the principal could make a general announcement. She couldn't tell if the system was working, and so she was playing with the knobs, working them, and said to herself, "I can't tell if I am on." Without dropping a beat, our young Romeo said, "Oh, yes, baby, you are on. You are always on."

I remember that I fell in love with my sixth grade teacher—funny, I cannot remember her name now. Some teacher's names you remember, yet hers I can't. But, I most distinctly remember seeing her over the summer after 6th grade and she was immensely pregnant. I still remember the jealousy that I felt and the thought, "How could you do that to me!" Ah, yes, we love our teachers.

Speaking of teachers reminds me of one disastrous time when—like most fathers probably try to do—I offered to take the girls to school. This would have been unusual since—because of surgery—I usually get up at 5 AM and am out the door by 6 AM at the latest, sometimes earlier. Yet, on this day when the girls were in the lower school, I must have been off and decided to be a really good dad. Yeah. I am sure that Paula was quite amused just at this prospect as it was. I may be a doctor, but I am certainly not capable of taking care of children.

Collecting the girls into our old, Chevrolet woody station wagon, Paula reminded me as we left the house that "Caroline needs to sit up front, because she has a queasy stomach." So, my girls pick their seats, and off we go. First, we stop to get Caroline and she does not sit up front as Paula had recommended, but picks a seat in the middle (remember, this is one of the old station wagons with the third seat facing backwards). Then, it is off to get Kristen and Robbie. However, I look at the gas gauge and see that we are running low on gas and I pull into a station. I give Cecily $20.00, which in those days was more than was needed, and told her, "Tell the guy that I want $5.00 of gas." So, I am pumping and pumping and then I realize—I have to fill up the entire tank because he took the money and she didn't give him the message. My mood started deteriorating.

Now, we get up to Robbie and Kristen's and they load in the car and sort of obliquely say, "Caroline is sitting in the middle?" But, I ignore them. And, then it is off to get our last packet, Caryn. Unfortunately, I just sort of knew where Caryn lived and the girls had said that they knew the way. Big mistake. Very big mistake. And, this is pre-GPS era. So, we are driving around this development until finally—by some divine intervention, if there is some god up there who looks after hapless fathers—we stumble on her house and the girls say, "That looks like it." Last pickup accomplished.

So, off we go to the school on a beautiful fall day—actually it was Halloween. The air was crisp and wonderful and I had "The Monster Mash" playing loudly on the radio. So, we are on this narrow two-lane road, behind some truck that I cannot pass and no shoulder and Caroline says, "I feel sick." I said, "Caroline, just hold on—I will pull over. Just give me a minute." Suffice it to say that Caroline did not give me a minute or even a second. There was just screaming from the middle seat and kids piling over the front seat and further to the rear seat.

Finally, I was able to find a place to pull over and in the left passenger well Caroline had emptied her stomach contents, Cheerios, milk, you name it—I think there was pizza in there. It was almost filled up and spilling over into the next section. And, Caroline looked like some sort of hound dog, white pale face, dark circles under her eyes. No one would sit in the middle so they all had to adapt. Caroline started complaining but I said, "Caroline—there is no other place for you and it is your vomit. Just scoot over—you can't have anything else left in you."

So, our unlikely band of Canterbury pilgrims resumed our quest, aiming for the promised land of the Day School. However, now the chorus was not "The Monster Mash," but "I am cold" when I lowered the windows or, "It stinks in here," when I rolled them up. I was so happy to drive up to the school. In those days they had an art teacher who always used to wear different hats when you pulled up and he would open your doors for you. So, Daingerfield was wearing his chicken hat that day and he opened the doors and the kids split instantaneously. I muttered bitterly, "I don't know why they disappeared like that," and he poked his head in the car and said, "Oh, I think I do."

Well, I pulled over to call Paula from the office, to complain—we were supposed to go hiking on my day off and I had visions of cleaning vomit out of my car. About that time, Carter appeared and said, "Teacher says that I am in trouble because I don't have my homework." I thought about it and told Carter, "Go tell teacher that your homework is covered by vomit in my car. If she wants it, I will bring it to her." After a few minutes Carter returned and said, "Teacher says it is OK, Daddy." And, by the miraculous phenomenon that exists in our small community, Caroline's Mom heard through the network—she was "in"—what had happened and by the time I got home she had arranged for a special cleaning service to take care of "the issue." God, I never knew there was a service for cleaning vomit out of cars but I was sincerely thankful that there was such an entity.

> *Mothers have to remember what food each child likes or dislikes, which one is allergic to penicillin and hamster fur, who gets carsick and who isn't kidding when he stands outside the bathroom door and tells you what's going to happen if he doesn't get in right away. It's tough. If they all have the same hair color they tend to run together.*
>
> *Erma Bombeck*

2 May 2009

> "... I've seen it around the world, in the poorest countries and in countries riven with conflict, ... It is women who are the key to breaking out of poverty, breaking out of stagnation. ... It's women who can contribute to achieving real security—not bombs and bullets and repressive governments."
>
> *Queen Noor*

Dear Dinah,

I don't know if I ever told you about my trip with Interplast to Honduras in the mid-1990. Interplast is a group which had its origins at Stanford in the late 60's, founded by Dr. Laub who was head of plastic and reconstructive surgery there. It focuses on treating burns and cleft palate and lip abnormalities in third-world countries. Their other goal is to train local physicians instead of just "doing cases" for the locals. Sort of the teaching a man to fish philosophy. I guess that I learned about it because some of my pals from Penn had gone on to be faculty members at Stanford and had done some Interplast trips—piquing my interest.

My trip was a two-week mission. I remember flying down through Tegucigalpa and then on to San Pedro Sula. I was disappointed at the time that we wouldn't be working in the historic capital of the country, but as it turned out, we worked so hard that that was an irrelevant consideration. I was the last to arrive since most of the others had arrived en mass from Northern California. They were dressed suitably as Californians, in shorts and flip flops, while I incongruously enough arrived in a blue blazer and tie. Quickly shed, for no other reason but survival in the heat.

The first couple of days were arranged so that the pediatricians could assess children and some adults for surgery while those of us who would be involved in the surgeries would prepare the OR's. I developed my first appreciation for the people of Honduras and their stoicism during this period. Many of them had walked for days to come and have their children assessed. There was a seemingly endless queue and yet there was never any murmur of complaint or irritation. Once the list had been selected the other patients and family members disbanded without any anger. They knew that Interplast would return in 3 months, but more than that, there was an acceptance of fate, of life that I have never seen in the U.S. I have a phenomenal respect for these people.

People of Indian or Native American blood have the highest incidence of cleft palate disease. Therefore, in Honduras you see things that you would just never see in the U.S. because of the population in conjunction with the limited healthcare resources. For males it can be slightly better than females because they can grow mustaches and hide some of the shame of their diseases. However, many of these patients historically have been kept in back rooms as shameful reminders of some punishment the family believes is being visited on the family.

By treating cleft palate and lip disorders in these communities, you are not only treating a medical problem, but you are treating the whole patient—reassimilating them into the community, changing in a fundamental way their entire life. Moreover, the way that their family and their community treats them will be forever altered. Interplast will treat older adults but it tried on my trip to concentrate on younger patients because the long-term effects would be amplified. Moreover, the time for speech therapy and social integration to work was vastly improved.

The operating room in which we worked was set up with three anesthesia machines. You could reach from one to another quite easily—this was essential because we didn't take breaks and if you did have to leave for an instant (if nature called) one of the other two anesthesiologists could watch your patient. Typically, we would board a collection bus around 5 AM and get to the hospital, assess the patients and start working around 7 AM. We would work until around 7 PM. The surgeons—like all surgeons—wanted to work later. However, they forgot in their calculation that we were getting to the hospital about an hour before they were and also we had to spend two hours recovering the patients in the recovery room, so we wouldn't finish until 9 PM. So, that became a non-negotiable point.

The other thing that we dealt with was complaints about turnover. This is the big issue in healthcare generally, even in the third world. I remember we had to wash off the equipment to reuse it and also mop the floors, change everything between cases. So, one world-famous plastic surgeon complained to me about the turnover and asked what we could do about it. I said, "Well, here is a mop. You could also scrub all of this equipment." After that, he didn't ask me about turnover anymore. Generally, however, everyone was very much into the pitch-in mode.

Everyone was housed with private families. I stayed in a compound which was exceptionally luxurious, behind moderately high walls but not excessive. The house was very nice, even by American standards, but the garden was magnificent—blooms everywhere. I was puzzled by the fact that all of the other houses on the block had private security, usually two or three teenage boys with an automatic weapons sitting on lawn chairs outside of the walls. Ours didn't have a private security force, though. When I asked about this, I was told that my host—some guy who was of Lebanese extraction and was a hyper-successful businessman in the city—was very close to the regime and that no one would dare touch his house. At least, if they wanted to live.

One of my good friends there was a Honduran anesthesiologist. I remember he drove a beautiful old-model bright red Mercedes convertible. One day he asked if I would like to see his family's hospital and I had to admit that I did. So, we tooled over there and entered something completely different than the public hospital where we had been working. Private rooms. Nurses in uniforms with caps. It seems that he came from a large family and he was an anesthesiologist. His brother was a general surgeon. One other was an obstetrician. Another was an internist. I am sure that some other specialties were covered. But, they had their own—quite successful—hospital and clinic to boot! Nepotism works when you keep it in the family.

One night, we were all taken to some amazing home in the hills overlooking San Pedro Sula. The people who owned it had the most magnificent library overlooking the twinkling lights of the city and they had a grand piano centrally located in the library. We were entertained to a short concert and then had the most wonderful cocktail party that I could recall—primarily because of the setting. I was told at the time—even then—that no one could ever again build a home where they did right up in the hills. It was built at time when you could build there, but since then, no one else was permitted to build structures there. So, that made that evening even more special.

On the Saturday night when the mission was completed, the medical community in San Pedro Sula had a big dance in one of the local halls in our honor. Once again, my northern Californian cohorts appeared, perhaps not in flip flops but decidedly not dressed for a dance in a Latin country. Meanwhile, I—per usual—appeared with my blazer and tie. First, this is just what I would do to show respect to my host. Second, I might not know much but—could it be our New Mexican upbringing?—I know enough to know that in Latin America that how you dress does connote something about your station.

So, while the other guys were wallflowers all night, I got to dance the night away. All of the beautiful young girls in the city were there, all dressed to a fair-the-well, most elegantly. In particular, I had more than one dance with an exceptional dark haired and eyed beauty in a Pokka dot dress. I am sure by this time that I had had more than my fair share of cocktails, but I didn't care when she said, "You know, you really don't dance badly for an American." I was in heaven. I am sure that my Spanish was fluent that night, too.

> *"I was recently on a tour of Latin America, and the only regret I have was that I didn't study Latin harder in school so I could converse with those people"*

Dan Quayle

3 May 2009

"What do I know about sex? I'm a married man"

Tom Clancy

Dear Dinah,

It is indisputable that you pick up lots of stories after you have practiced medicine for a long time. Some tug on your heart strings. Others are quite amusing and of these amusing stories it is also indisputable the many of these have a sexual component.

When I was an intern in Chicago—going back as far as that—I remember one woman who came into my clinic. She was generally healthy, but when it came time to really find out what the problem was she told me that she had a "powerful itching in her kit-cat." Well, I might have gone through medical school at that point but it took me a little time to determine exactly what her kit-cat was. Soon enough I ascertained what the crux of the matter was. I explained that I was not a kit-cat doctor and sent her to one of my partners over at the Lying-In hospital. It seems, as I could well understand, that she was suffering from crabs.

Another patient—a very obese woman—who had been in my clinic for a year when I was an intern became pregnant. Quite earnestly I asked her how she did this—we had become quite close and this was long before the days of bariatric sensitivity. She said, "Do you really want to know?" Of course I did, so she said that when she and her husband were amorous she would get up on a table and use a broomstick to hold her stomach back so that he could "perform the deed." To this day, that image has never left me. And, I sincerely hope that he never disappoints her because if he does, she merely has to release the broomstick to have him flying across the room.

On the South Side of Chicago a large percentage of my patients were black and I really learned a great deal about southern culture from them even before I ever lived in the south. There are some phenomenal books on The Great Migration which occurred out of the South from 1915 to 1930. One of the habits, traits, peculiarities of the region that they brought with them to Chicago and that I learned about was pica. Many of my patients told me that they had to go home every couple of years or so—at the most—to get some clay to chew on and eat. "Clay from anywhere else just don't taste the same, Dr. Boggs." I drink a great deal of mineral water and can discern the difference between a Perrier, a San Pellegrino, a Saratoga and so on. Well, I can imagine that the same applies to clay and these patients of mine really craved the taste of home.

As an anesthesia resident, I didn't acquire the same stories—at least not right up front. In fact, I can still remember to this day that the first few months of anesthesia training were the most stressful days of my life. In medicine you might have a lot of admission and an incredible amount of work. However, in the OR—until you become attuned to the way patients respond to anesthesia and surgery in general, I at least was at the edge of my seat every minute. I was never sure if their next heart beat might not be their last. Gradually, you do develop a feel for what is good and what is not but when you have no baseline you—or at least I—lived in fear.

I do recall one case when I was in Philly. This young male came in with a nail through his testicle. They sent me to pre-op him. So, patiently I took his very straightforward history and then gave him his anesthetic options—either a spinal or a general anesthetic. Completely straight-faced, he looked at me and said, "Oh, but I don't want anesthesia." I do not know what the long-term result was but I am sure the psychiatrists were called.

When I was in the Air Force, I was sitting in the anesthesia office at Malcolm Grow the day before Thanksgiving. Everyone else had gone home and I was by my lonesome. A very attractive and smartly dressed woman came by with a baby carriage, knocked on the door and asked if I was with the anesthesia department. I said that I was. She said that she had a postoperative complication and I asked her to sit down so that I could see what we could do.

She explained that she had had a thumb pinning by one of the orthopedists a few weeks before. However, the pin was still in her thumb and she had been having problems. I asked her to elaborate. "Well, every since the operation my sister-in-law has been trying to impregnate me with cosmic rays from outer space. I have tried to keep my hand in the microwave to protect myself but I just can't do this all the time." By this time I was sitting up quite straight. She was contentedly pushing the stroller back and forth.

"Well, you know, we actually see this not infrequently," I told her. Unfortunately, I am not a specialist in this particular area but I have a partner in the building who has handled this before. "You aren't going to call the psychiatrists, are you?" she asked me. "No, I want to call the specialists for this particular problem." I dialed psychiatry and said, "We have a woman here who needs your particular expertise. Yes, that is right.

We are in the anesthesia office." Soon enough, two very large orderlies came to collect her. However, she did not seem either surprised or distressed to see them.

Over the years in South Carolina I have had hundreds of amusing stories. If I had to cull one particular group for you, thought, I would mention the dildoes. We have removed light bulbs. We have taken care of perforations. And, some can be quite dramatic. In one case a guy had managed to get one of those bumpers that keeps a boat from bumping against a dock up his butt. I still am unclear of the exact process if for no other reason than the sheer dimension. But, I can assure you—in this particular case it most definitely did not come out the way it went in. It was so large that we had to "birth it" like a C-section, removing it abdominally.

Another case was a gentleman who came in having a heart attack. He needed emergency heart surgery but before he was put to sleep some information was gleaned. He admitted to having a very large wooden dildo up his butt—we think this might have been associated with his infarction. And, his last words before going to sleep were, "Don't tell my wife." So, the cardiac procedure was completed successfully and then a general surgeon was summoned. He used the vacuum extractor from OB to deliver the dildo—this time it was able to be removed the way it had gone in. I do not know if the man's wife was ever informed as to the precipitating cause of MI.

Other interesting things that we encounter are piercings. One concern about piercings is that if they are left in place and electrocautery is used, a burn can result. I remember one girl who had—according to the nurses—the most dramatic labial piercing that they had ever seen. I asked her to remove it and she declined, stating that "it will just seal up before the operation is over." I really didn't think this would happen but I also wanted to be equitable. So, I said, "Well, if you will just sign this release stating that we are not responsible if you get a third-degree burn down there, then we will let you leave it in." I have rarely seen someone move so quickly to remove something, blindly, under the sheets.

My favorite piercing story was of a handsome young guy who came in with his entire face covered with tacks, pinning's, studs, you name it. One of our older surgeons with a pronounced southern drawl looked at me and said, "Looks like he had an accident with a tackle box, don't it?"

"Cock-a-doodle-do! Any cock will do!"

Carole Lombard

4 May 2009

> *"After the first glass, you see things as you wish they were. After the second, you see things as they are not. Finally, you see things as they really are, and that is the most horrible thing in the world."*
>
> Oscar Wilde

Dear Dinah,

 I think that if I really had to admit it, I am sorry that I never got to try "The Green Fairy," or absinthe as it were, before I stopped drinking. It seems to be making a comeback, being cleared for sale in Europe and the U.S. (even) again. There is such an aura about the drink—the color, the effect, the inspiration. When everyone from Verlaine and Rimbaud to Voltaire and Hemmingway raves about something, it must have some merit. Yet, recent discoveries seem to point to the fact that it is not the wormwood—in fact—which causes the strange hallucinatory effects of absinthe, but rather the extraordinarily high alcohol concentration. And, that I don't need.

 Visiting Paris, I have seen amusing drunk stories. One morning while Paula and I were sipping on our coffees and eating croissants at a café, we saw this guy stumble over to a bank of bicycles and just vomit all over them. I do not believe that the evening had ended for him, at least not until a few minutes right before that. So, while he was standing there, catching his breath from his exhausting—and I might say exhaustive—performance, a perfectly coiffed, meticulously dressed gentleman (as only a continental can so do) came up and surveying the situation gently tapped him on the shoulder, indicated that the bicycle which he had vomited upon was now required and then politely removed it from the rack. Speculation can run amok about how this would play in the U.S., but I can give you thirty scenarios and this is not one of them.

 Speaking of perfect coiffures, you have two daughters so I am sure that you will relate to this situation. Paula and I visited Cecily while she was studying at Science Po and Carter came down from Germany where she was living at the time. Paula had been "working" with her hair for a while. It is one of those situations where a wise husband knows when to lay low.

For example, it might be the perfect length and Paula will ask me, "What do you think about me getting it all cut off?" Well, I might voice my opinion and say what I think, but when push comes to shove and she shows up at night shorn like the back of a recently shaved sheep, I know my marital duty. "God, you look so cute!" I do not consider such a lie a disqualification for heaven and purgatory per se would be better than the purgatory of a straightforward answer.

Nonetheless, Cecily dragged us to her appointment—so much fun to share, sitting in a French hair salon—and she was chatting away in French with the stylist. He conversationally asked her about Paula's hair (in French) so that we were spared the details. However, it later emerged that the conversation went something like this. "Who does your mother's hair?" "Well, right now she has someone back home." "Well, I hope she isn't paying too much for that!" Ah, the delicacies of the French.

Paula was particularly pleased since we were all in economic saving mode so that—guess who—could live in an apartment in the 7th arrondissement! Nonetheless, as soon as Carter arrived the girls enacted a plan. I remember distinctly that we were walking out by the Obelisque at the Place de la Concord when each girl grabbed one of Paula's arms, held her and said, "Mommy, we are going to have a *hair intervention.*"

On a more somber note, I have to tell you about one of my favorite museums and areas in Paris. While the Louvre is indisputably the place I have to make a pilgrimage to whenever I go to Paris—and, the way that Paula and I do it is usually to do a few hours on several days instead of all in one day, because I get glassy-eyed after a more than a couple of hours, no matter how wonderful the art is—my secret love is the Musée Nissim de Camondo. In a way, it is analogous to the Frick in New York in that you can actually see some wonderful art and decorative pieces in situ. You feel more as if you have visited a private home after going there than as if you had spent the afternoon in a museum.

The history of the museum is rooted in tragedy. The Camondo's were a wealthy Jewish banking family and moved in the late 1800's from their home in Istanbul to Paris. They were so wealthy in fact that they were called "the Rothshields of the East."

His only son, Nissim—for whom the museum is named and whom Moïse expected to take over the family bank—was killed as a Lieutenant in the Aéronautique Militaire in aerial combat in Lorraine during World War I. He was buried in the Montmartre Cemetery. Moïse never quite recovered from this, withdrawing to his home which he donated to the French government following his death in the 30's.

Unfortunately, during World War II, his daughter, Béatrice, his son-of-law Léon Reinach and their children, Fanny and Bertrand died in the Nazi camps. The story is that Beatrice was quite a horsewoman and put to shame a Nazi officer at an exhibition during the war. Perhaps not an intelligent thing to do; maybe she thought that her family's money would protect them, which it did not. So, the entire Camondo family died out.

The house, residence, museum—whatever you wish to call it—was modeled on the Petit Trianon at Versailles. Without reservation, it is a stunning edifice, rather understated from the street and only dramatic when you enter its grand hall and see its views over the Parc. I would not bore you with a recitation of the things that you could find in the residence but would tell you about the things that really struck me.

First, downstairs off of the enormous dining room—where Moïse used to entertain his gourmand friends even after he went into seclusion following his son's death—is the porcelain room, where all of the various services were stored. This is a very bright, sunny room and the guides told us that as he aged, Moïse took more and more of his meals in this small cabinet instead of the dining room. The plates are covered with botanical themes, decorated with birds, animals or other wildlife. It is a very comfortable and inviting nook in a very grand house.

Second, without a doubt, the library cannot fail to make an impression of you. If I recall correctly—and it has been a few years since I have been there—the paneling for the room was from an older room and was "retrofitted" into the new structure so as to fit. It is elegant simplicity.

The final feeling that I had, as did Paula, on our tour of the residence was that we were really left alone to soak up the atmosphere. I believe that the afternoon when we toured the mansion there were two other couples. This is in comparison to possibly two or three museum staff members per floor. We were able to pause, reflect, examine and deliberate over each of the exquisite objects in whatever rooms we wanted to. It was as if we were in your home and you had to run out—I expect that we were probably more intrusive than we would have been in your house. But, maybe not! So, despite the sadness associated with the Camondo line, they have bequeathed to France a rare jewel that can be savored by the traveler willing to get off the beaten path.

So near—and yet in both feel and period, light years apart—is the Musée Cernuschi. This museum is also located right off of Parc Monceau, but concentrates on Asian art. In fact, it is the 5th oldest Chinese art museum in Europe. Particularly, though, I have never seen so many glazed Tang horse works in my life. Typically, a museum might have one or two, usually in the rather conventional poses. In this museum I saw riders and horses in poses which I had never before associated with the Tang period—a fluidity, spontaneity and artistic quality which I was unaware of. The collection is exhaustive and we spent hours looking at just this part of it. And, to cap it off, the museum has the largest Buddha that I have ever seen before, not having been to the orient.

Leaving museums for a while, though, Parc Monceau is always a treat. Here you can really see Parisians enjoying the beauty of their city. Whenever we have been there—regardless of the season—we have seen mothers out with their children. And, this parc is certainly most inviting. It has many meandering lanes and ways which you can wander off on, along ponds, some waterfalls and sculptures of long-forgotten luminaries. In addition, there are some wonderful architectural treats to see, such as the rotunda, Corinthian columns, and bridges. Since it is in the English style instead of the more strict French style, it is a bit more welcoming. Yet, typically French, it is planted and trimmed to perfection.

I will close with a few lines from Rimbaud for you. It is from his poem, "A Season in Hell," which is my favorite:

> Once, if my memory serves me well, my life was a banquet where every heart revealed itself, where every wine flowed.
>
> One evening I took Beauty in my arms—and I thought her bitter—and I insulted her.
>
> I steeled myself against justice.
>
> I fled. O witches, O misery, O hate, my treasure was left in your care!
>
> I have withered within me all human hope. With the silent leap of a sullen beast, I have downed and strangled every joy.
>
> I have called for executioners; I want to perish chewing on their gun butts. I have called for plagues, to suffocate in sand and blood. Unhappiness has been my god. I have lain down in the mud, and

dried myself off in the crime-infested air. I have played the fool to the point of madness.

And springtime brought me the frightful laugh of an idiot.

Now recently, when I found myself ready to croak! I thought to seek the key to the banquet of old, where I might find an appetite again.

That key is Charity.—This idea proves I was dreaming!

"You will stay a hyena, etc . . .," shouts the demon who once crowned me with such pretty poppies. "Seek death with all your desires, and all selfishness, and all the Seven Deadly Sins."

Ah! I've taken too much of that:—still, dear Satan, don't look so annoyed, I beg you! And while waiting for a few belated cowardices, since you value in a writer all lack of descriptive or didactic flair, I pass you these few foul pages from the diary of a Damned Soul.

"*Cities have sexes: London is a man, Paris a woman, and New York a well—adjusted transsexual.*"

Angela Carter

5 May 2009

> *"Behavior is a mirror in which every one displays his own image"*
>
> *Johann Wolfgang von Goethe*

Dear Dinah,

I do not know if it is Paula's basic kindness or her relative innocence, but she exerts a powerful draw for certain guys in the community. Unfortunately, they are not the ones which you might want to attract—else, I might not be so amused. But, if Paula ever wanted to create her own harem I have not doubt that she would be able to do so. What to call a harem of men? Well, since harem means hidden, I guess it would still apply. Tragically, for Paula's group, they might have what we call here in the south "summer teeth." Some are here, some are there.

I think the first case of someone in Gaffney being totally smitten with Paula was when we were having the wrought iron work done on our house. This was a young guy, an excellent worker at that time. He told us of one horrible story from Spartanburg. Apparently, one of the doyens of Spartanburg society arranged to have some incredibly detailed wrought iron gates made for her estate. However, when came time to accept them, she refused to take them and refused to pay for them. The poor guy who had spent hours of effort designing them, working on them and putting material into them was forced to take them to the scrap yard. Where, as it turns out, the "lady" went a few days later and purchased them for pennies on the dollar.

Well, anyway this guy was lonely and would chat with Paula before he would start working on the fence, the balconies and the gates at our house. Paula would speak to him for a while but did have to limit the conversation. However, he kept getting back to some stories, one in particular, where a certain woman would only let him "polish her finials." He would try to send other people out to do this, but she only wanted him. I told Paula that I thought that he might be suggesting that he might want her to polish his finial, so it was just as well that he was finishing the job.

That turned out to be a close call as it were. This guy had an absolute middle age meltdown, left his wife and two adorable boys and ran off with a woman on the lamb from the FBI. First, the fled to the lower part of the state, but ultimately they were caught in a KOA campground in

North Carolina. Since he had finished our left and middle balcony right before this all happened, we thought that we might end up with a very asymmetrical house. I think that last balcony might have been his last piece of honest work—before license plates, that is.

Another time, we had to have someone come and seal our marble in the bathrooms. Paula called her friend at the tile place in town and they sent over a guy, I will call him "Greg." Greg finished sealing all of the surfaces and then started telling Paula about how his wife was up in Alaska. Then, he came up with what I personally consider the best pickup line I have ever heard. He said that he was doing breast cancer research—with a completely straight face according to Paula—and he would love to give her a free examination.

She told me that she was alone in the house with him at the time and didn't want to make him do something crazy. So, she just declined the study—probably he didn't have all of his informed consent forms with him. He persisted but finally relented. But, he said, "Well, I'm not leaving unless I get a hug." So, she hugged him. When her friend Kathy heard this she screamed! But, Paula had one objective and that was to get him out the door. Kathy and I did insist that she call the tile store and tell them about her "experience" with Greg, so that other women might be spared.

Not all of these treats come from workers. Paula has also worked on the board for a local charity. There was an elderly gentleman who really didn't do much on the board, but was on it for various reasons. Well, he used to come by and Paula would have coffee with him. Then, one day he tried to give her a kiss. So, she had to stop Mr. X. from coming by. However, I believe in this particular case he did quite well, having a large bevy of other women with whom he "coffeed."

I must add that this man is in contradistinction to our friend, Oscar, who has headed the Habitat board and now works with Paula on the Cherokee County Rehabilitation Board. Oscar is a gentleman such as they just don't make anymore. In addition to that, he is purported to be retired but if he is retired, I don't know how hard he worked when he was full-time! He spends all of his days doing community service, literally from the crack of dawn to late at night. Sometimes we have to call-screen his calls because he never stops.

What Paula and Oscar have been up to most recently has been obtaining funding from the state for people who own their own homes but have insufficient income to replace bad windows, leaky roofs and decrepit porches. They do the groundwork with some local contractors and file grants with the state to get these monies. You have never seen such genuine appreciation in most applicants. Certainly, most are deserving. A few have tried to game the system but overall it seems like an excellent and efficient system. One problem case Paula had was a woman with more money than she could account for. However, while never stated directly it appeared that the woman was a "working girl." I don't know if they were able to get her income low enough to qualify—I doubt it.

Personally, I have never had the luck with ladies like Paula has had with "her guys." I think the only case that I can remember hearing about was one day, Paula went to Wal-Mart to get something right after I had gone there—it was a weekend and I generally refuse to set foot in the place on a weekend but it must have involved a project. Well, the clerk had remembered my name and when Paula checked out she said, "Are you related to Steve Boggs?" Paula said, "Yes," and then the young clerk went on and on about how cute I was and how disappointed she was that I was wearing a ring and that she had thought about writing my number down from the check. Paula cut that transaction short and told me about it, smiling when she said, "And, she was a little heavy and just not that cute." Touché!

Another night, I did return home to find the most wonderful phone message on the machine. It was a woman with the sultriest black voice I have ever heard and if you had to say someone was in heat, this would be her. I could only—at best—paraphrase for you at this distant juncture, but it went something like this: "I know you're there and I know what I like and you're packing it. You've got something to give me and I've got a treat for you. I will be in the red dress with a long slit up the side, sitting, sipping on a Manhattan at Ichabod's. I will be waiting for you. Come and get your treat."

Well, I dialed the number—I still remember we had just returned with the girls, they were relatively young at the time. I said, "Excuse me, I think you might have left your message on the wrong machine." There was a long pause and then, "click." I think—knowing what I know now, being older and wiser, that I should have at least driven to Ichabod's and bought her a drink.

Q. Is your Dad a terrorist?

R. No, why?

A. Because, you are the bomb!

May 6, 2009

Conclusion—written at 30,000 feet over what some call the *"fly-over states,"* between Mississippi and Pennsylvania

"Who travels for love finds a thousand miles not longer than one."

Japanese Proverb

Dear Dinah,

It seems somehow appropriate that I bring this series of letters to a conclusion from an indeterminate location. Realistically, on life's paths we are all—in one way or another—in our own personal quantum orbits, travelers who really never know where we are. I might not be mathematically or scientifically correct, but I think from a poetic and spiritual perspective that this is closer than further from the truth.

Now, I am getting ready to start on my new job—and, I must say that I am quite eager to do so. However, I must say that I am sad that I will not have the time to write as frequently as I have for the past two months. I will—I can promise—continue to send you stories, anecdotes and amusing tidbits. They will just not be with the frequency with which I have been sending them up to now.

I cannot tell you what a process this has been for me—as I know it has for you. When I received the first email about your medical situation from Jim I was absolutely devastated. You are the closest person to me, in age and experience, whom I know. Our families courses have been inextricably intertwined and you and I spent so much of our youth together.

Paula and I have frequently remarked how fortunate we have been. Until our 40's, neither of us really had any significant tragedies in our lives. For me, the loss of Dad about 10 years ago was somewhat of a relief with him suffering from Alzheimer's in the last few years of his life. I did lose two partners to cancer which really struck home, but my relationship with them—while very close—was nothing like the sort of friendship that you and I have had.

Each day, I wrote to entertain you, to amuse you and to tell you a story. It only came to me—when I realized that I would be starting my new job and had to conclude this break in my life and this undertaking—that in essence these letters had become love letters of a kind. Love is such a denigrated and misinterpreted term. It doesn't always have to be romantic nor passionate in the sense which we usually associate with it. Yet, it does have to have a particular intention toward an object, a focus, to exist.

My focus has been to think of you and also of my past in a unique way each day while I have been writing to you. I am astounded at some of the things that I have remembered. I have also developed a deep sense of gratitude for the life which I have been given. I might not ever have been a master of the universe nor succeeded in certain ways. But, I have realized that my path has been strewn with the most fascinating, interesting characters placed here by God to influence me in one way or another. And, now, they have not only been here for me but also for you. Perhaps they have given you a sense of the wonder and uniqueness of the life which you have led also.

If we are to literally interpret the biblical thought that a man's years are—generously—to be three score and ten, then I realize that I have less than one score left. All I can do is to try to make each, singular, unique day which I am left with the best that it can be. I do not find this particularly morbid, because as the Buddhists say, the only person who is prepared to live is the person who has concentrated on his death.

Likewise, I cannot tell you how appreciative I am of the fact that you are doing so well. It makes me so happy, it makes my heart dance to think that you have survived this trial—and trial it most certainly has been—for yourself, your family and all of your friends. I eagerly await seeing you in the near future. Until then, I wish you:

> Many long, happy afternoons,
> The enjoyment of many children's graduations,
> Much happiness with Jim,
> Driving your car with abandon,
> Indolent deserts,
> The sun on your cheeks,
> The wind in your hair,
> A 'con brio" heart,
> And grass stains on your toes.

With this I conclude my letters to you, dear Dinah, and send you this final poem.

Sonnet 104

To me, fair friend, you never can be old,
For as you were when first your eye I eyed,
Such seems your beauty still. Three winters cold
Have from the forests shook three summers' pride,
Three beauteous springs to yellow autumn turned
In process of the seasons have I seen,
Three April perfumes in three hot Junes burned,
Since first I saw you fresh which yet are green.
Ah yet doth beauty like a dial hand,
Steal from his figure, and no pace perceived.
So your sweet hue, which methinks still doth stand,
Hath motion, and mine eye may be deceived.
For fear of which, hear this, thou age unbred:
Ere you were born was beauty's summer dead.

William Shakespeare

Steve and Mom, April 1959

Steve and Dinah, Easter, April 1959

Steve, Dinah and Steve's Dad

Paula, Jim, Dinah, Steve and Carter at Jim and Dinah's wedding
—Carter was flower girl

Carter's christening in Philadelphia, Dinah was her godmother.

Families around 1996

Steve and Dinah, July 2011

INDEX:

Absinthe	185
Alzheimer's	103, 105, 195
Anderson, Jon	10
Anglican Church	21
Art Institute of Chicago	211
Astonished	45
Atatürk, Mustafa Kemal	75
Auden, W. H.	129
Austin, Jane	11, 167
Barreca, Regina	27
Barry, Dave	161
Berlin, Germany	14
Berlioz, Hector	102
Bierce, Ambrose	140, 149
Biggers, Jeff	165
Bird, Sue	81
Bishop, Jim	136
Bobick, Michael	23
Bombeck, Erma	21, 177
Boy Scouts	173
Breast cancer	23, 30, 39, 80, 160, 192
Brussels, Belgium	124, 127
Butterfield, Betty	21
Cantor, Tim	30
Capretz, Pierre	79
Carroll, Lewis	29
Carter, Angela	190
Cattle	59
Channing, William Ellery	93
Chicago, Illinois	11, 27, 29, 36, 43, 48, 71, 72, 73, 82, 93, 94, 105, 116, 138, 145, 165, 170, 182, 190

Chicago, University of	211
Chickens	17, 19
Churchill, Winston	124,
Cicero, Marcus Tullius	157
Clancy, Tom	182
Clarissa, or the History of a Young Lady	11
Cleft palate	178, 179
Cocteau, Jean	160
Connor, Tim	32
Conrad, Joseph	71
Coquís	151
Coyoacán, Mexico	69
Cracker Barrel Restaurant	21, 22
Cranmer, Thomas	21, 23
CSS (Cansei de Ser Sexy)	101
Dali Lama, The	88
Dangerfield, Rodney	169, 172
Daniel Boone National Park	165
Davies, Michael	118
de Balzac, Honoré	11, 22, 141
de Cervantes, Miguel	41
de Gotari, Carlos Salinas	67
de La Hoya, Oscar	14
de Lamartine, Alphonese	7
de Montaigne, Michel	25, 40, 123
de Nerval, Gérard	119
Dementia	34, 35, 103, 105, 119
Disney, Walt	106, 119
Doe's Eat Place	115, 117
Donne, John	64
Dostoevsky, Fyodor	11
Down's Syndrome	47
Durst, Will	114
Earthwatch	133, 134
El Moro	150
Eliot, T.S.	61, 97
Epicurus	147

Faulkner, William	36, 168
Forester, Edward Morgan	39
Foxworthy, Jeff	103
Frazier, Ian	57
French garden	25
French in Action	77
Friendship	39, 61
Frogs	17, 19
Frost, Robert	49
Gaffney, South Carolina	17, 19, 29, 36, 37, 61, 63, 74, 75, 80, 88, 115, 117, 140, 141, 145, 146, 159, 166, 174, 191
Gandhi, Mahatma	76, 105
Ganskopp, Daryl	20
Goldstein, Adam	152
Graves, Robert	133
Guadalupe Hidalgo, Treaty of	68
Guilt	6, 32, 45, 50, 51, 68, 98, 112, 142
Gyms	43
Hairy Cell Leukemia	93
Harvard University	21
Hayek, Selma	69, 70
Hedges	26
Holiday, Billie	95
Illegal immigrants	67
Interplast	178, 179
Irish	10, 11, 159
Istanbul, Turkey	7, 8, 10, 138, 187
Ivre	12
Izzard, Eddie	21
Jay, Billy	60
Jewelry	31
John, Elton	42, 161
Juanes	15

Jury Duty	49, 50, 51, 52
Kahlo, Frieda	69
Keith, Toby	128
La 5a Estacion	14, 15
La Casa del Frances	151
La Oreja de Van Gogh	15
La Residencia, Mallorca, Spain	134
Lake Shore Drive (LSD)	71
Languages, foreign	48, 77
Latin pop	14, 15, 16
Lauer, Matt	3
Lehrer, Thomas	105
Les Troyen	102
Lewis, Huey	53
Little Black Dress (LBD)	34
Lombard, Carole	184
Love, Actually	109
Mallorca, Spain	133, 136
Marijuana	3, 90
Marinol	3, 4
Marlowe, Christopher	73
Mas'udi, Masdar	9
Mathematics	42, 169
McCormick's Bookstore	116
Medical licenses	26
Mencken, Henry Louis	87
Merton, Thomas	87, 88
Metropolitan Museum of Art	101
Mexico City, Mexico	16, 68, 71
Mississippi, Greenville	87, 115, 116, 117, 118
Mississippi, Jackson	33, 101
Mohr, Jay	133
Montreal, Canada	23, 80
Mosque, Blue	8
Mother Teresa	25
Munich, Germany	36, 80

Musée Cernuschi	188
Musée Nissim de Camondo	187, 188
Muzzy	
Nabokov, Vladimir	153
New Mexico, University of	211
New York, New York	1, 11, 36, 90, 101, 149, 187, 190, 211
Nicknames	17
NKVD (Narodnyy komissariat vnutrennikh del)	69
Noonan, Peggy	90
Noor, Queen	178
North Dakota	57, 58, 60
O'Malley, Austin	156
Outward Bound	161
Oxford University	133, 135
Paige, Satchel	17, 44
Parc Monceau	188, 189
Parker, Dorothy	56
Peaches	11, 140
Peachoid	140
Pennsylvania, University of	211
Perpignan, France	79
Phelps, William Lyon	163
Philadelphia, Pennsylvania	57, 145,
Philips, Emo	45
Puerto Rico	149, 150, 151, 152
Quayle, Dan	173, 181
Ramadan	8
Raye, Colin	105
Rice University	22, 104
Rivera, Diego	69
Roberts, Michael	16
Rye, New York	211

San Diego, California	30, 41, 100, 101
San Francisco	27, 36
San Miguel de Allende, Mexico	68, 138
Savannah, Georgia	10, 27
Science Politiques (Science Po)	185
Seattle, Washington	27, 80
Shakespeare, William	48, 92, 197
Shaw, George Bernard	52
Sheep	59, 187
Shelley, Percy Bysshe	119
Shriner, Will	111
Sigma Chi Fraternity	54
Smith, Elinor Goulding	85
Spears, Britney	36
St. Louis, Missouri	90, 91, 211
St. Patrick's Day	10
St. Tropez, France	126
Stalin, Joseph	69
Stanford University	11, 178, 211
Steinbeck, John	21
Stewart, Jon	139
Still (alcohol)	75
Stilson, Jeff	82
Sultanahmet, Istanbul	8
Syntex	16
Tabb's BBQ Restaurant	116
Tea	53
The Cloisters	101
Thoreau, Henry David	36, 74
Torpedo Baby	5
Tours, France	27, 79, 80
Tree of Death	30
Trotsky, Leon	69
Turkish bath	7
Twain, Mark	42, 108
Updike, John	127

Venegas, Julieta	14
Vieques, Puerto Rico	151, 152
Virginia, University of	21, 53, 157
Voltaire (Arouet, François-Marie)	143, 185
von Goethe, Johann Wolfgang	80, 191
Von Willebrand's Disease	93
Warren, Robert Penn	115
Washington University, St. Louis	211
Waugh, Evelyn	106
Webelos	41
West, Mae	35
Wilde, Oscar	33, 185
Wilder, Thornton	99
Wilkes-Barre, Pennsylvania	149, 161
Williams, Robin	90
Wright, Stephen	144
Yale University	79
Zeon's paradox	25
Zócalo, Mexico City	16

BIOGRAPHICAL INFORMATION:

Steve Boggs:

Born and reared in Albuquerque, New Mexico, Steve lived there through his graduation from Manzano High School. Thinking that he was going "East" to school, he was a Chancellor's Scholar at Washington University in St. Louis, graduating Summa Cum Laude. He received his medical degree at the Pritzker School of Medicine at The University of Chicago, completed an internship in Internal Medicine at the Hospitals of University of Chicago Hospitals and did his residency in anesthesiology at The University of Pennsylvania.

Following training, he was on active duty with the USAF as a Captain and then a Major in the Medical Corps. He was on staff at Malcolm Grow USAF medical center and Bethesda Naval. He was also Assistant Professor of Anesthesiology a the military medical school, The Uniformed Services University of the Health Sciences.

Upon separation from the military, he and his family moved to South Carolina where they lived for over 20 years. He was Chairman of Anesthesiology at Spartanburg Regional Medical Center in Spartanburg, SC and also President of Foothills Anesthesia Consultants. He served as Vice-Chairman of Anesthesiology for The Geisinger Health System in Wilkes-Barre, PA before joining his current practice.

Presently, he is a member of Ramapo Anesthesia, a group of over 70 anesthesiologists and over 25 CRNA's. He works at various hospitals about an hour outside of New York City. He and his wife, Paula, live in Middletown, NY and frequently return their house in Gaffney.

Aimee Wise:

Born and raised in Spartanburg, SC, Aimee studied various aspects of art at the School of the Art Institute of Chicago and graduated in 2008 with a B.F.A. in Visual Art. She and her dog, Baloo, currently reside in Lafayette, Colorado. To see more of her work, you can visit her website at www.QueenEtheria.com.

Dinah Howland:

Dinah Howland attended elementary school through high school with Steve in Albuquerque. After finishing her undergraduate studies at the University of New Mexico, she attended Stanford University and received a Masters in German Literature. She then worked in Europe for Bain and Company. Returning to the US, she received her MBA from Harvard and worked as a consultant with McKinsey. Currently, she resides in Rye, NY with her family.